Section 504:

Civil Rights for the Handicapped

by

Richard Clelland

Published by
AMERICAN ASSOCIATION OF SCHOOL ADMINISTRATORS
1801 North Moore Street
Arlington, VA 22209

© Copyright, 1978

Stock No. 021-00327
Price: $4.95
2-9 copies, 10 percent discount
10 or more copies, 20 percent discount.
Orders for less than $15 must be accompanied by payment in full and add $1.00 for handling and postage.

Contents

Foreword

Introduction

Chapter I
Introduction to Title V, Section 504.. 1

Chapter II
Employment Practices 7

Chapter III
Program Accessability 72

Chapter IV
P.L. 94-142 and Section 504: Comparison and Contrast 102

Chapter V
Future Issues 110

Appendix A 113

Footnotes 124

References 128

About the Author... 128

Introduction

On September 26, 1973, the Rehabilitation Act of 1973 became Federal law. Title V, Section 504 of the Act reads, "No otherwise qualified handicapped individual in the United States . . . shall, solely by reason of his handicap be excluded from participation in, be denied the benefits of, or be subjected to discrimination under any program or activity receiving Federal financial assistance." The significance of Section 504 is that it is the first major statutory civil rights enactment that protects handicapped individuals from discriminatory practices in employment and educational opportunities, and in accessibility to Federally supported programs and activities. The congressional intent of Section 504 is identical to the nondiscrimination provisions of Section 601 of Title VI of the Civil Rights Act of 1964 (discrimination based upon race) and Section 901 of Title IX of the Education Amendments of 1972 (discrimination based upon sex), and, like those enactments, establishes a Federal government policy against discrimination in all Federally assisted programs and activities.

However, while congressional intent of Section 504 is identical to Titles VI and IX, the Department of Health, Education and Welfare emphasizes that Section 504 statute and regulation differs conceptually from both Titles VI and IX.

> The premise of both Title VI and Title IX is that there are no inherent differences of inequalities between the general public and the persons protected by these statutes and, therefore, there should be no differential treatment in the administration of Federal programs. The concept of Section 504, on the other hand, is far more complex. Handicapped persons may require different treatment in order to be afforded equal access to Federally assisted programs and activities, and identical treatment may, in fact constitute discrimination. The problem of establishing general rules as to when different treatment is prohibited or required is compounded by the diversity of existing handicaps and the differing degree to which particular persons may be affected. Thus, under Section 504, questions arise as to

when different treatment of handicapped persons should be considered improper and when it should be required.

Serious administrative decision-making problems exist for all recipients of Federal financial assistance because (a) the concepts underlying Section 504 are new and complex, and (b) there are few judicial, legislative, or administrative agency interpretative precedents concerning implementing the statute and regulation. For public school administrative decision-makers, the lack of substantive Federal guidance in implementing Section 504 requirements can be both frustrating and costly. Public school administrators who have had the responsibility of transforming Titles VI and IX from legislative statute to specific administrative policy and practices are acutely aware of the intricate and often subtle complexities involved in affecting social change within public schools and local communities. This fact was recognized by the Department of Health, Education and Welfare in the development of regulation for Section 504.

> The most important problem which has hindered the development of [Section 504] regulation is the constant need to weigh competing equities while resolving complex issues. Thus, while we recognize that the statute creates individual rights, the statute is ambiguous as to the specific scope of these rights. Implicit in this situation is the need to assess carefully the overall impact of a particular requirement both on the persons protected by the statute and those regulated by it.[1]

Written as a companion document for the American Association of School Administrator's handbook *Public Law 94-142: Special Education in Transition*,[2] the purpose of this handbook is to (a) examine the statutory and regulatory requirements of Section 504, and (b) to delineate the various dimensions of local educational agency administrative responsibilities relative to the successful implementation of various Section 504 subparts. The goals of this handbook are similar to the four goals of *Public Law 94-142: Special Education in Transition:*[2] (a) to inform public school administrators of the statutory and regulatory requirements of Section 504, (b) to identify critical issues and delineate possible problem areas relative to Section 504, (c) to describe the effect that Section 504 could have on organizational structure and operations, and (d) to examine the effect that Section 504 could have on administrative decision-making concerning the assessment and evaluation of criteria for program effectiveness and efficiency. To achieve these goals, the handbook is divided into five chapters. These chapters are:

- Chapter I, Introduction to Title V, Section 504. Chapter I emphasizes (a) an overview of Title V, (b) an overview of Section 504 regulation, and (c) the salient substantive and procedural issues addressed by Section 504 regulation.
- Chapter II, Employment Practices. Chapter II emphasizes (a) the developmental history of Section 504 regulation concerning employment practices, (b) a delineation of specific regulatory requirements, and (c) staffing issues relative to the structure and operation of local educational agencies.
- Chapter III, Program Accessibility. Chapter III emphasizes (a) the

developmental history of Section 504 regulation concerning program accessibility, (b) a delineation of specific regulatory requirements, and (c) program accessibility issues relative to the structure and operation of local educational agencies.
- Chapter IV, P.L. 94-142 and Section 504: Comparison and Contrast. Chapter IV emphasizes the substantive and procedural similarities and differences of P.L. 94-142 and Section 504.
- Chapter V, Future Trends. Chapter V identifies possible future trends concerning (a) employment practices, (b) program accessibility, and (c) delivery of educational services to handicapped and nonhandicapped individuals.

The two caveats used in *Public Law 94-142: Special Education in Transition* are appropriate for this handbook. First, this handbook is not intended to be a comprehensive planning document for the successful implementation of Section 504. Second, this handbook does not examine all the possible organizational structure and operation changes that may be necessary to implement Section 504. While the salient components of Section 504 are presented, a comprehensive examination of each requirement of the regulation is neither feasible nor necessary. In response to these limitations, the goals of this handbook will be achieved if: (a) the reader is more aware of the various dimensions of administrative decision-making necessary for successful planning, and (b) the suggested program planning, conducting, and analyzing activities recommended by the author facilitate service delivery effectiveness and efficiency.

With these two limitations in mind, Chapter I provides a basic introduction to the historical and philosophical development of Section 504.

Chapter I

Introduction to Title V, Section 504

Overview of Title V[1]

Title V of the Rehabilitation Act of 1973 contains five sections, four of which relate to affirmative action for handicapped individuals, and one (Section 504) which relates to remedial action, voluntary action, and self-evaluation. Section 501 deals with employment of handicapped individuals in agencies and departments of the Federal government. Section 502 establishes an Architectural and Transportation Barriers Compliance Board. Section 503 covers employment under Federal contracts and Section 504 prohibits discrimination by recipients of Federal financial assistance.

Section 501

Section 501, Employment of Handicapped Individuals, requires development of affirmative action programs for employment of handicapped individuals in departments and agencies of the executive branch of the Federal government. Section 501 is administered by the U.S. Civil Service Commission.

There have existed for a number of years in many Federal agencies, programs designed to employ individuals with handicaps. Section 501 expands and strengthens these efforts by requiring each department and agency of the Federal government to develop and implement affirmative action programs to hire, place, and advance in employment handicapped individuals. These plans and reports on the success of the programs are submitted to the Civil Service Commission annually for review and approval. In its report to Congress for fiscal year 1975, the Civil Service Commission reported that,

> The biggest forward step was taken last year when processes were initiated to carry out statutory requirements for the implementation of affirmative

action program plans for the hiring, placement, and advancement of handicapped individuals and disabled veterans. This new thrust has provided the mechanism for integrating the program into regular personnel management operations of all Federal agencies.

Now, it is timely to reflect on how well the program has been doing after one full year's experience in carrying out the new focus for affirmative action. Overall, we have observed a considerable increase in the interest and commitment to the program among agencies. One major accomplishment has been the development of an awareness by non-handicapped persons toward the capabilities, employment problems and needs of handicapped individuals. This awareness has resulted in positive actions being taken to assure that goals and objectives are reached. Agencies have addressed these issues with varying degrees of commitment.

Some agencies have done an excellent job in ensuring that the program is well integrated into their personnel management systems. This has resulted in measurable achievements. Some agencies have treated the program with a "special emphasis" focus which has had both favorable and unfavorable results. In some instances, we found desirable results occurred where there had been little action previously. In other cases, we found that the program is still being viewed as a "paper exercise" and very few real accomplishments have been observed.

Section 501 also establishes an Interagency Committee on Handicapped Employees, co-chaired by the Secretary of Health, Education and Welfare and the Chairman of the Civil Service Commission. The purpose of the Committee is to provide Federal and other employment of handicapped individuals, and to review, in cooperation with the Civil Service Commission, the adequacy of hiring, placement and advancement practices with respect to handicapped individuals in the Federal service. Reporting to Congress on the Committee's activities in fiscal 1975, the Civil Service Commission stated,

> The activities of the Interagency Committee on Handicapped Employees have been very helpful in providing direction and making recommendations. The Committee has tapped the expertise of many representatives in several Federal agencies to work on its goals and objectives. Emerging from their efforts have been concrete suggestions and recommendations aimed at identified problem areas. It is expected that this wide use of interagency talent will have a firm and lasting government-wide impact on the affirmative action program.

Section 502

Section 502, Architectural and Transportation Barriers Compliance Board, establishes within the Federal government a board which will deal with architectural, transportation, and attitudinal barriers confronting handicapped individuals, particularly in public buildings and facilities, surface transportation, and residential and institutional housing. The Architectural and Transportation Barriers Compliance Board is composed of the heads (or their designees) of: (a) the Department of Health, Education and Welfare, (b) the Department of Transportation, (c) the Department of Housing and Urban Development, (d) the

Department of Labor, (e) the Department of the Interior, (f) the General Services Administration, (g) the U.S. Postal Service, (h) the Veterans Administration, and (i) the Department of Defense.

The Compliance Board is charged with the responsibility of ensuring compliance with standards developed under P.L. 90-480, The Architectural Barriers Act of 1968, which requires all buildings and facilities constructed using Federal funds to be accessible to physically handicapped individuals. Also, the Compliance Board investigates and examines methods of eliminating architectural, transportation, and attitudinal barriers confronting handicapped individuals, and reports to the President and Congress on ways of eliminating these barriers.

Section 503

Section 503, Employment Under Federal Contracts, requires that any Federal government contract or subcontract ($2,500 or more) for the furnishing of supplies or services, or for the use of real or personal property, including construction, must contain a provision requiring affirmative action by the contractor to recruit, hire, and advance in employment qualified handicapped individuals. Contractors with a contract of $50,000 or more and with 50 or more employees, must prepare and maintain an affirmative action program at each establishment which sets forth policies, practices, and procedures for operation. This section is administered by the Department of Labor through its Office of Federal Contract Compliance Programs under regulation issued on April 16, 1976.

State vocational rehabilitation agencies and rehabilitation facilities are specifically mentioned in the Department of Labor regulation. The applicable provisions are:

- The contractor should enlist the assistance and support of recruiting sources (including state employment security agencies, state vocational rehabilitation agencies or facilities, sheltered workshops, college placement officers, state education agencies, labor organizations and organizations of or for handicapped individuals) for the contractor's commitment to provide meaningful employment opportunities to qualified handicapped individuals;
- The contractor should establish meaningful contacts with appropriate social service agencies, organizations of and for handicapped individuals, vocational rehabilitation agencies or facilities, for such purposes as advice, technical assistance and referral of potential employees;
- An effort should be made by the contractor to participate in work-study programs with rehabilitation facilities and schools which specialize in training or educating handicapped individuals;
- Contracts with sheltered workshops do not constitute affirmative action in lieu of employment and advancement of qualified handicapped individuals in the contractor's own work force; and
- The Director of the Office of Federal Contract Compliance Programs shall use his or her efforts, directly or through contractors, subcontrac-

tors, local officials, vocational rehabilitation facilities, and all other available instrumentalities, to cause any labor union, recruiting and training agency or other representative of workers who are or may be engaged in work under contracts and subcontracts to cooperate with, and to assist in, the implementation of the purposes of the Act.

Federal contractors are to identify all employees and applicants for employment who believe themselves covered by the law. This necessitates a voluntary system for self-identification of the presence of a handicapping condition, particularly with respect to present employees. Information obtained in this fashion must be kept confidential and can be used only in accordance with the Act. Employees with handicaps who refuse when requested to voluntarily provide employers with information concerning their handicaps, may not do so at any future time.

Section 504

Section 504, Nondiscrimination Under Federal Grants, prohibits discrimination against qualified handicapped individuals in Federally assisted programs or activities solely on the basis of handicap. Section 504, therefore, includes all programs supported by Federal monies in areas such as employment practices, elementary, secondary, and higher education, building accessibility and provision of health and social services. In general, Section 504 includes the entire Federal grant-awarding structure and covers persons with handicaps in a variety of ways, i.e., in discrimination in the provision of services, denial of benefits, or exclusion from participation on the basis of handicap.

Overview of Section 504 Regulation[2]

Section 504 regulation was published in the *Federal Register* on May 4, 1977. The regulation is divided into seven subparts. Subparts A, General Provisions, defines the important terms that are used throughout the regulation and states in general terms the discrimination acts that are prohibited. Subpart A also sets forth what the Department of Health, Education and Welfare believes is a simple, workable system of administration, including: (a) assurances of compliance, (b) self-evaluation by recipients, (c) establishment of grievance procedures, and (d) notification of employees and beneficiaries of the recipient's policy of nondiscrimination on the basis of handicap. The regulation covers all types of physical and mental impairments, including drug addiction and alcoholism.

Subpart B, dealing with employment practices, bars discrimination by recipients of Department of Health, Education and Welfare assistance in the recruitment, hiring, compensation, job assignment and classification of qualified handicapped individuals, and in the provision of fringe benefits. Subpart B also requires employers to make reasonable accommodation to qualified handicapped applicants or employees unless it can be demonstrated that the accommodation would impose an undue hardship on the employer.

Subpart C sets forth the central requirement of the regulation—program accessibility. All new facilities are required to be constructed so as to be readily accessible to and usable by handicapped persons. Every existing facility need not be made physically accessible, but all recipients must ensure that programs conducted in those facilities are made accessible. While flexibility is allowed in choosing methods that in fact make programs in existing facilities accessible, structural changes in such facilities must be undertaken if no other means of assuring program accessibility is available.

Subpart A, B, and C of the regulation, as well as Subpart G—which incorporates by reference the Department of Health, Education and Welfare's procedures under Title VI of the Civil Rights Act of 1964—apply to all recipients of financial assistance from the Department. The remaining subparts of the regulation contain more specific requirements applicable to three major classes of recipients.

Subpart D is concerned with preschool, elementary, and secondary education. Its provisions have been closely coordinated with those of the Education for All Handicapped Children Act of 1975 (P.L. 94-142). Both Section 504 and P.L. 94-142 regulation require that recipients operating public education programs provide a free appropriate education to each qualified child in the most normal setting appropriate. Subpart D regulation also sets forth evaluation requirements designed to ensure the proper classification and placement of handicapped children, and due process procedures for resolving disputes over placement of students. While the Department of Health, Education and Welfare does not intend to review individual placement decisions, it does intend to ensure that testing and evaluation procedures required by the regulation are carried out, and that school systems provide an adequate opportunity for parents to challenge and seek review of these critical decisions. And the Department of Health, Education and Welfare will place a high priority on pursuing cases in which a pattern or practice of discriminatory placements may be involved.

Subpart E concerns postsecondary education. It proscribes discrimination against handicapped persons in recruitment, admission and treatment after admission. Colleges and universities are required to make reasonable adjustments to permit handicapped persons to fulfill academic requirements, and to ensure that they are not effectively excluded from programs because of the absence of auxiliary aids.

Finally, Subpart F deals with health, welfare and other social service programs. Subpart F forbids discrimination in providing such services and requires larger recipients to provide auxiliary aids to handicapped individuals when necessary. Specific provisions require hospitals not to discriminate against drug addicts or alcoholics who need medical services and to establish emergency room procedures for communication with persons with impaired hearing. Under Subpart C, health and social service providers may satisfy their program accessibility obligations with respect to existing facilities by arranging to meet beneficiaries in accessible locations. In addition, small providers may refer patients or other beneficiaries to accessible providers as a "last resort" alternative to making significant structural changes.

The remaining chapters of this handbook are concerned with the three subparts pertinent to local educational agencies (i.e., Subparts B, C, and D).

Chapter II

Employment Practices

Subpart B of Section 504 regulation prohibits recipients of Department of Health, Education and Welfare financial assistance from discriminating in the recruitment, hiring, compensation, job assignment/classification, and fringe benefits provided qualified handicapped individuals. Subpart B also specifies that employers (e.g., public school systems) must make reasonable work environment accommodations for qualified handicapped applicants or employees unless demonstrable evidence can be provided that accommodation would impose an undue hardship on an employer. This prohibition of employment discrimination is applicable to *all* recipients of Department of Health, Education and Welfare financial assistance, including state, intermediate, and local educational agencies. Furthermore, any state, intermediate, or local educational agency that receives assistance under The Education of the Handicapped Act must take "positive steps" to employ and advance in employment qualified handicapped individuals in educational programs assisted under that Act.

Schneider has defined staffing "as the processes involved in identifying, assessing, placing, evaluating, and developing individuals at work."[1] These processes are integral to educational administrative decision-making relative to recruiting, selecting, appraising, and promoting administrative, direct, and support service personnel in local educational agencies. By emphasizing that staffing occurs within the confines of local educational agencies, the impact of the characteristics of organizational decision-making, structure and operation on the staffing processes can be examined concerning the contribution handicapped and non-handicapped individuals make to the attainment of local educational agency goals. The objective of staffing procedures is to identify those variables that affect an individual and relate to his or her behavior at work.

Schneider states that there are two important points concerning staffing procedures:

- The staffing procedures of an organization invariably constitute the first

contact most individuals have with the organization. Therefore, the ways in which the staffing processes are carried out may be important determinants of individual attitudes toward the organization; and
- While staffing procedures are designed to identify individuals who will be able and willing to do a job well, it is important to remember that the issue is to identify how well a person will do in a particular organization context. Thus, the long-range design of the staffing process is to identify attributes of individuals, but the process itself is based on the context of the working environment which includes job and organizational characteristics.[2]

There are two major classes of employee behavior that are of interest when evaluating the success of staffing programs. First, employee satisfactoriness, which is individual employee contributions to an organization such as high performance, low absenteeism, and low turnover. Second, employee satisfaction, which is individual employee evaluation of the rewards (e.g., money, security, prestige, or self-worth) received from performing and obtaining organizational goals. Again, Schneider notes that,

> It should be noted that employee satisfaction has not been considered a goal to be achieved . . . when staffing organizations. The concentration has been instead of the contributions people make to the attainment of organizational goals (satisfactoriness). Both kinds of criteria (employee satisfaction and satisfactoriness) are important. First, because of the growing concern for the quality of work life, and second, for very practical reasons that (a) satisfied workers tend to be less prone to turnover and absenteeism . . . and (b) organizations, by rewarding people for their contributions to goal attainment, can create a more satisfied work force.[3]

The issue of transforming Section 504 employment practices regulation into local educational agency operations "involves organizational policy toward both achieving production criteria (satisfactoriness) and also facilitating the attainment of the objectives of its human resources (satisfaction)." With reference to local educational agency organizational philosophy, Section 504 regulation strongly implies that "emphasis on individual performance alone is an unworkable model for social organization." As Gardner suggested several years ago,

> Extreme emphasis on performance as a criterion (of status) may foster an atmosphere of raw striving that results in brutal treatment of the less able, or less vigorous, or less aggressive; it may penalize those who undeniable excellences do not add up to the kinds of performance that society at any given moment chooses to reward.[4]

Two basic assumptions the author proposes are:
- To successfully implement Section 504 employment requirements, public school personnel must understand the role of job and organizational analysis in the staffing process; and
- The procedures and techniques employed in job and organizational analysis are not only appropriate for qualified handicapped workers in educational employment situations, but appropriate for all workers, regardless of the type of work involved or the unique cognitive, affec-

tive, or physical characteristics of any individual worker.

The remaining portion of Chapter II examines:
- The developmental history of Section 504 employment practices regulation, including (a) legislative history and (b) judicial history;
- Specific regulatory requirements, including (a) reasonable accommodation, (b) employment criteria, and (c) preemployment inquires;
- Staffing issues relative to the structure and operation of local educational agencies, including (a) development of policy statements, goals, and objectives, (b) evaluation of current personnel procedures (i.e., architectural barriers needs assessment and the role of job and organizational analysis in the staffing process), (c) employing a self-evaluation coordinator, (d) development of a self-evaluation plan, (e) implementation of the self-evaluation plan, and (f) monitoring and evaluation.

Developmental History of Section 504 Regulation: Legislative History[5]

With the passage of the Smith-Fees Act (P.L. 66-236) in 1920, vocational rehabilitation for the handicapped began. Enacted to provide training opportunities to handicapped World War I veterans, the Act had no substantive history, procedural guidelines, or theoretical basis for service delivery. Four services were delineated in the Act: (a) vocational training, (b) counseling, (c) prosthesis, and (d) job placement. This limited number of services remained as the only ones available until an expansion occurred in 1943.

In 1936, the Randolph-Sheppard Act (P.L. 74-732) authorized the states to license qualified blind persons to operate vending stands and concessions in Federal buildings. Subsequent locations of the vending stands and concessions have been expanded to include non-Federal buildings. Although the Randolph-Sheppard Act specified the blind as operators of the vending stands, the categories of clients qualified to receive vocational rehabilitation services remained restricted.

With the passage of the Barden-LaFollette Act (P.L. 78-113) in 1943, the entire field of vocational rehabilitation significantly changed. The handicapped clients and services provided, the available money, and the purpose of vocational rehabilitation changed. It expanded so that clients could be furnished any services deemed necessary to prepare them for employment. Furthermore, for the first time, the mentally ill and the mentally handicapped were included as recipients of vocational rehabilitation services. Funds were made available to provide clients with medical, surgical, and other physical restoration services required to eradicate or alleviate disabilities. The authorized services included surgery and therapeutic treatment, hospitalization, transportation, occupational licenses, tools and equipment, prosthetic devices, maintenance during training and other goods and services. With this Act, the separate state agencies established to serve the blind came into the state-Federal vocational rehabilitation program.

Another milestone in the growth of the legislative basis of vocational rehabilitation occurred with the passage of P.L. 83-565, the Vocational Rehabilitation Amendments of 1954. Two important provisions were included in P.L. 83-565: (a) funds were available for vocational rehabilitation counselors training grants, and (b) funds were available for the alteration or expansion of existing rehabilitation facilities and workshops.

Activities in this area continued for another 11 years until the Vocational Rehabilitation Amendments Act of 1965 (P.L. 89-333) broadened the Federal vocational rehabilitation program. P.L. 89-333 amendments provided: (a) funds for a 75-25% matching ratio for Federal support, (b) for construction of new facilities, and (c) extended evaluation of clients. Individuals falling within one or more of fifteen categories of disability were able to receive up to eighteen months of extended evaluation to determine their rehabilitation potential. If a client had any disability other than those fifteen, six months was the limit for evaluation. Three years later, P.L. 90-341 amended the Vocational Rehabilitation Act by extending the basic program to include follow-up and services to family members.

P.L. 93-112, the Rehabilitation Act of 1973 (as amended by P.L. 93-516) broaden the scope of rehabilitation substantive and procedural issues to: (a) include basic civil rights issues (i.e., employment practices, educational opportunities, and program accessibility), (b) changed the basic focus of vocational rehabilitation so that the most severely handicapped are the priority category of clients for receiving vocational rehabilitation services, and (c) placed more emphasis on job placement activities.

From a historical perspective, the Rehabilitation Act of 1973 follows in the general civil rights movement requiring equal employment opportunity and affirmative action. The following acts and executive orders provided impetus for the current Section 504 regulation:

- The Equal Pay Act of 1963. All employers subject to the Fair Labor Standards Act are required to provide equal pay for men and women performing similar work. In 1972, coverage of this Act was extended to an estimated 15 million additional executive, administrative, and professional employees.
- Title VI of the Civil Rights Act of 1964. Discrimination is prohibited based on race, color, or national origin in all programs or activities which receive Federal financial aid. Discrimination is also prohibited if a primary purpose of Federal assistance is the provision of employment. Revised guidelines adopted in 1973 by 25 Federal agencies prohibit discriminatory employment practices in all programs if such practices cause discrimination in services provided to program beneficiaries.
- Title VII of the Civil Rights Act of 1964. Title VII prohibits discrimination because of race, color, religion, sex or national origin in any term, condition or privilege of employment. The Equal Employment Opportunity Act of 1972 greatly strengthened the powers and expanded the jurisdiction of the Equal Employment Opportunity Commission in enforcement of this law. As amended, Title VII now covers: (a) all private employers of 15 or more persons, (b) all public and private educational institutions, (c) state and local governments, (d) public and

private employment agencies, (e) labor unions with 15 or more members, and (f) joint labor-management committees for apprenticeship and training.
- Executive Order 11246 (as amended by Executive Order 11375). Issued by President Johnson, this order requires affirmative action programs for minorities and females by all Federal contractors and subcontractors. It also requires that firms with contracts over $50,000 and with 50 or more employees develop and implement written programs which are monitored by a Federal agency.
- The Age Discrimination in Employment Act of 1967. Employers of 25 or more persons are prohibited from discriminating on the basis of age against persons 40 to 65 years of age in any area of employment.
- Title IX, Education Amendments of 1972. Extends the coverage of the Equal Pay Act and prohibits discrimination on the basis of sex against employees or students of any educational institution receiving Federal financial aid. The provisions covering students are similar to those of Title VI of the Civil Rights Act of 1964.
- Vietnam Era Veteran's Readjustment Assistance Act of 1974. Discrimination is prohibited and affirmative action programs for the hiring, placement, and advancement of disabled veterans are required under provisions similar to Title V of the Rehabilitation Act covering handicapped individuals.
- The National Labor Relations Act and Related Laws. Discrimination on the basis of race, religion, or national origin may violate rights arising under these laws. It is unlawful for employers to participate with unions: (a) in the commission of any discriminatory practices unlawful under these Acts, (b) to practice discrimination in a manner which gives rise to racial or other divisions among employees, and (c) to practice discrimination to the detriment of organized union activity. It is also unlawful for unions: (a) to exclude individuals discriminatorily from union memberlship, thereby causing them to lose job opportunities, (b) to discriminate in the representation of union members or non-members in collective bargaining, in processing of grievances, or in other respects, (c) to cause or attempt to cause employers to enter into discriminatory agreements, and (d) to otherwise discriminate against union members or non-members.

These laws and executive orders form the legislative civil rights environment as it exists today. Title V of the Rehabilitation Act promotes and expands employment opportunities for persons with handicaps. Congressional intent appears to be clearly aimed at initiating employment opportunities for persons with handicaps in the public and private sectors of the economy. To this extent, Title V becomes a part of the overall civil rights environment.

Developmental History of Section 504 Regulation: Judicial History

Subpart B not only follows the employment practice provisions of specific legislative and administrative statutes and regulations, but also extends to the handicapped a variety of judicial decisions and opinions concerning discriminatory employment practices. Because there is extensive judicial activity in this area (e.g., Hazelwood School District v. United States, decided in June, 1977), a comprehensive examination of recent judicial decisions is necessary for understanding possible legal responses to Section 504 regulation.

Weckstein has observed that legal challenges to testing, including employment testing, are based upon an examination of "the interaction between the procedural issues of testing and more substantive questions involved in classification."[6] In general, this examination involves a two step procedure:
- The first step in most challenges to the use of testing involves a prima facie showing of discriminatory impact of the testing system; and
- Upon such a prima facie showing, the burden shifts to those doing the testing to make some demonstration of the rationality of the testing procedures.

Court cases involving the "substantive questions" of classification are, in general, based on plaintiff's claims of denial of equal protection as guaranteed by the Fifth and Fourteenth Amendments. These cases primarily concern interests relevant to employment practices and student placement in educational programs, although judicial review of testing practices has been extended to jury selections and violations of Federal statutory enactments. Regardless of the specific interest being reviewed, the courts have been consistent in applying the two step procedure described by Weckstein. Therefore, equal protection standards applicable to employment opportunities are also applicable to jury selection procedures, Federal statutory regulations, and special education placement.

The prima facie showing of discrimination usually involves the traditional "suspect" classifications recognized by the courts. Alleged discrimination is usually based on race, ethnicity, sex, and now, the handicapped. "All that is required for this prima facie case is that the testing procedures produce significant statistical disparities between the percentage of the group represented in the particular classification and its percentage in the total testing population, and there need be no evidence of any discriminatory intent."[7] Several cases have enumerated this approach. In Chance v. Board of Examiners (1972), plaintiffs argued for a motion for preliminary injunction restraining the Board of Examiners of the City of New York from conducting examinations for supervisory positions in the New York City school system and from using these examinations as the basis for selecting supervisors. Plaintiffs claimed that the competitive examinations given by the Board of Examiners to those seeking permanent appointment to supervisory positions discriminated against blacks and Puerto Ricans and, thus, violated the Equal Protection Clause of the Fourteenth Amendment. In Bridgeport Guardians, Inc. v. Members of the Bridgeport Civil Service Commission (1973), plaintiffs challenged the constitutionality of hiring and promotion procedures employed by the Bridgeport, Connecticut Police Department. In according an injunction order "requiring the city to hire and promote blacks and Puerto Ricans from a pool of candidates qualified" for such positions, the court stated,

Where passing rate for 568 white applicants on patrolman's examination was 58 percent whereas passing rate for 76 black and Puerto Rican applicants was 17 percent, so that passing rate for whites was 3½ times the rate for blacks and Puerto Ricans, a prima facie case of de facto discrimination was established in respect to examination, even if there was evidence that difference in passing rates was due in large part to quality of schooling received by applicants.[8]

In the precedent setting class action suit of Griggs v. Duke Power Company (1971), Negro employees of the Duke Power Company "brought a class action against their employer . . . alleging that the employer violated the Civil Rights Act of 1964 by requiring a high school diploma and a satisfactory intelligence test score for certain jobs previously limited to white employees, so as to preserve the effects of the employer's past racial discrimination."[9] In granting plaintiff's relief, the United States Supreme Court held that,

> Under Section 703 of the Civil Rights Act of 1964, which forbids any employer to limit, segregate, or classify his employees in any way which would deprive or tend to deprive any individual of employment opportunities or otherwise adversely affect his employee status, because of race, color, religion, sex, or national origin . . . , an employer is prohibited from requiring a high school education or passing of a standardized general intelligence test as a condition of employment in or transfer to jobs when . . . both requirements operate to disqualify Negroes at a substantially higher rate than white applicants.[10]

The Supreme Court further held that,

> Under Title VII of the Civil Rights Act of 1964 . . . practices, procedures, or tests neutral on their face, and even neutral in terms of intent, cannot be maintained if they operate to freeze the status quo of prior discriminatory practices."[11]

With the absence of a showing of discriminatory intent, or de jure segregation, few courts have employed the "strict scrutiny" standard of review in cases involving the procedural issues of testing. In general, the courts have demanded some demonstration of the rationality of the testing procedures." Although this demonstration has utilized a variety of terms, a basic requirement is that there be some "demonstrable" and "rational" relationship between the "attributes" or "constructs" being measured by a test and the significance of these "attributes" or "constructs" in the performance of a specific task. In Chance v. Board of Examiners (1972), the court held that the "question was whether the examinations could be validated as relevant to the requirements of the positions for which they are given, i.e., whether they are job related." In Bridgeport Guardians, Inc. (1973), the court held that,

> Determining utility of an employment examination that is discriminatory in effect requires some consideration of standards applied in the field of psychological testing, namely, the criterion-related predictive validity approach involving the identification of criteria reflecting successful job performance and test scores and correlation of same with performance ratings of predetermined criteria, the construct validity approach involving an identification of "constructs" or characteristics, followed by a test

to measure degree to which applicant possesses required characteristics, and the content validity approach involving direct measurement of knowledge or skill needed for successful job performance.[12]

In Griggs v. Duke Power Company (1971), the U.S. Supreme Court held that the Civil Rights Act of 1964 "proscribes not only overt discrimination but also practices that are fair in form, but discriminatory in operation."[13] The Court elaborated upon this proscription by stating that the only appropriate employment testing should concern a "business necessity". Specifically, "if an employment practice which operates to exclude Negroes cannot be shown to be related to job performance, the practice is prohibited."[14]

While the above cases employed various terms to enumerate "rationality", "there have been two employment cases which have used strict-scrutiny language upon a prima facie showing of racially discriminatory effects without requiring any showing of discriminatory intent."[15] In Arrlington v. Massachusetts Bay Transportation Authority (1969), District Judge Garrity held that,

> Where use of general attitude test resulted in only 20% of black applicants as compared with 75% of white applicants being within first two-thirds of those to be offered positions and there was no evidence of any relevance to tests to duties of driver or collector for transit authority which did not disqualify any applicant because of low score on test, practice of offering employment to individuals in order of their performance on test was discriminatory.[16]

In Baker v. Columbus Municipal Separate School District (1972), Circuit Judge Dyer stated that "whenever the effect of a way or policy produces . . . a racial distortion it is subject to strict scrutiny [and] in order to withstand an equal protection attack it must be justified by an overriding purpose independent of its racial effects."[17]

"There has also been one case which declared that a testing procedure was a violation of equal protection without requiring any showing of racially or sexually discriminatory results."[18] In Armstead v. Starkville Municipal Separate School District (1972), the United States Court of Appeals held that,

> Where teachers' examination was not designed to and could not measure competency of teacher or even indicate future teacher effectiveness, and cut-off score would eliminate some good teachers, score requirement for hiring and retention of teachers was not reasonably related to purpose for which it was purportedly designed, and was violative of equal protection, whether or not it created racial classification.[19]

In general, it can be assumed that unless a testing practice can be "rationally" and "demonstrably" proven to be related to the objectives of a specific task, whether that task be job performance, classroom performance or any other form of criterion related behavior, it may be in violation of the equal protection clause of the Fourteenth Amendment, regardless of the level of judicial review employed.

"For the vast majority of cases involving a prima facie showing of discriminatory effect, the burden of justification requires a demonstration that the test measures what it purports to measure."[20] Specifically, when a test is used for classification or selection, "the test . . . must be shown to bear a strong relationship to categories being used, such as special education needs or successful employee traits and skills."[21] The courts have repeatedly proscribed:

- testing practices that fail to demonstrate test relevance to such "needs" or "traits and skills";
- the use of tests that "have been found to be irrelevant because [they were] designed for a different purpose"; and
- the use of tests that measure "different traits from those required for the job".[22]

The issue of proper validation practices to be employed in the classification or selection of individuals for educational placement or employment selection was first examined by the United States Supreme Court in Griggs v. Duke Power Company (1971). While the Court decided the interest of review under the *EEOC Guidelines on Employee Selection,* these same standards have been found to apply under the equal protection clause of the Fourteenth Amendment.

To date, the most extensive judicial examination of appropriate testing validation practices for employment selection has been enumerated by the United States Court of Appeals (Fifth Circuit) in United States v. Georgia Power Company (1973). On appeal from the District Court of the Northern District of Georgia, Circuit Judge Tuttle held that,

> Where [a] study to validate [an] employment test was . . . substantially at variance with the minimums of the EEOC validation guidelines and its premises also departed from the practices followed by [an] employer in the testing program as administered, [the] study's final induction of a positive correlation of test results vis-a-vis job performance was invalid.[23]

In recognizing the "complex and multi-faceted . . . aspects" of this case, Judge Tuttle expanded upon the precedent set by the U.S. Supreme Court in Griggs.

> In Griggs v. Duke Power Company . . . the Supreme Court held that the proviso of . . . Title VII of the Civil Rights Act of 1964 means that no test used for hiring or promotion is valid if it operates to exclude Negroes and cannot be shown to be related to job performance. Reversing the Court of Appeals . . . the Court decided that a test which excludes proportionately more blacks than whites from employment or advancement may be prohibited under the [Civil Rights] Act despite a lack of any discriminatory intent on the part of those developing and using the tests and in spite of professional origins of the test. Whereas in Griggs the company made no effort to prove that its tests were related to job performance, the appellee here introduced a mass of statistical data . . . by which it sought to prove a demonstrable relationship between test scores and job performance. On this appeal, we must resolve the question left unanswered by Griggs: What comprises an adequate demonstration that a company's testing program satisfies the proviso . . . [of] Griggs.[24]

More specifically, Judge Tuttle concerned himself with defendant Georgia Power Company's attempt at providing the court with a validity study that justified the employment selection and promotion practice utilized by the company.

> Georgia Power acknowledged its Griggs burden to validate the tests it had used with such racially discriminatory results and attempted to carry that burden with expert opinion evidence. This took the form of a post-testing study . . . which concluded that, after each of the tests had been properly weighted for the jobs involved, the resulting scores bore a positive relationship to job performance ratings by supervisors.[25]

In deciding that the proof provided by defendant Georgia Power Company was not sufficient to meet the standards articulated in Griggs, several important statements of dictum were enumerated:

- A test or other selection device may be shown to be "job-related" under Griggs only if the employer can demonstrate or manifest that the test reliably predicts which applicants possess the reasonably necessary job skills and traits;
- The most accurate way to validate an employment test is to administer the test to be validated to all applicants but proceed to select new employees without regard for their test achievement, and then, after an appropriate period of work experience, compare job performance with test score. An alternative is "concurrent validation", a process in which a representative sample of current employees is rated, then tested, and their job ratings compared with test scores;
- When can tests, which are shown to have discriminatory results, be used? We view the reference by the Griggs court to EEOC guidelines as an adjunct to the ultimate conclusion that such tests must be demonstrated to be job related. We do not read Griggs as requiring compliance by every employer with each technical form of validation procedure . . . Nevertheless, these guidelines undeniably provide a valid framework for determining whether a validation study manifests that a particular test predicts reasonable job suitability. Their guidance value is such that we hold they should be followed absent a showing that some cogent reason exists for non-compliance;
- The minimum standards recommended for validation strategy by EEOC guidelines . . . provide for differential validity. Data must be generated and results separately reported for minority and nonminority groups wherever technically feasible;
- Accepting arguendo that whites scoring high on [a] test perform satisfactorily [and] to conclude that therefore blacks scoring low could not adequately perform the same jobs [is] a nonsequitar . . . Griggs demands more substantial proof . . . of the relationship between test scores and job performance.[26]

"A distinction between content validity, in which the test measures characteristics found among persons in the particular job category, and predictive validity, in which performance on the test is related to actual job performance, runs through several of the cases."[27] A brief examination of these two "general principles" was enumerated in Chance v. Board of Examiners and Board of Education of City of New York (1971). Because of the court held that "the evidence with respect to the validity, reliability and objectivity of . . .

examinations" was to be examined in context of these "principles", delineation of the court's dictum is appropriate.

> It seems to be generally accepted that before an examination will be recognized as a reliable instrument for measuring the fitness and ability of a candidate to perform tasks demanded by a given position, the examination should be validated, i.e., shown to be reasonably capable of measuring what it purports to measure. The first step toward this basic objective is to insure that as to subject matter the examination will elicit from the candidate information that is relevant to the job for which it is given. If so, it is described as having "content validity".
>
> To a lesser extent the validity of an examination as a means of selecting candidates best suited for a position may also be checked or verified empirically by comparing the relative examination scores of successful candidates with their later performance on the job. If there is a significant correlation between test scores and later performance, the examination has "predictive validity".[28]

In general, judicial reviews of testing practices follow the EEOC guidelines in requiring determination of predictive validity whenever possible. However, if determining predictive validity is not feasible, content validity is held sufficient. Nonetheless, before content validity is held sufficient for an employment selection testing instrument, there must be "clear infeasibility of predictive validity." Chief Judge Dewitt in Fowler v. Schwarzwalder (1972) explicitly enumerated this point in granting relief to black residents of St. Paul, Minnesota who had brought a class action suit against the members of the St. Paul Civil Service Commission for employing a fire fighters test that was unfair to minority persons. In observing that the "principle issue . . . is the validity of the . . . test", Judge Dewitt stated that,

> Defendants sought to prove job relatedness or validity of the test through testimony of Civil Service personnel who prepared it and of the fire chief and fire department training officer. Their testimony tended to show that the test had content validity in that it sampled the knowledge, abilities and skills demanded of a fire fighter. An expert in the field . . . said that the job analysis was adequate, that the test had a high degree of content validity, and the questions effectively and fairly measure the abilities needed to succeed as a fire fighter.[29]

However, while Judge Dewitt recognized the high degree of content validity demonstrated by the Civil Service Commission, he noted that, "test validity generally means predictive validity or statistical evidence of validity and the content validity is acceptable only when predictive validity studies are not feasible."[30] In holding that defendants "have not shown the infeasibility of a concurrent or predictive validity study, the Court concluded that had not rebutted the prima facie case of discrimination in the content of the examination made out by the disparity in statistics, and enjoined defendants from employing persons on the eligibility list resulting from that examination from use of it in future examinations until it [had] been validated in accordance with . . . EEOC guidelines."[31]

Even if a high degree of predictive validity is achieved with an employment instrument, it does not necessarily follow that the employer has "adequately born the burden of showing that his examination has a manifest relationship to the employment in question."[32] As Weckstein observed concerning the Court of Appeals' decision in United States v. Jacksonville Terminal Company (1971), "a demonstrated correlation of high test results with job performance was inadequate validation in the absence of a similar demonstration of correlation between low test results and low job performance."[33]

One final point of importance has been recognized by the courts. "A test may be invalid because it measures, in terms of content validity, a very small number of traits involved in job effectiveness."[34] In Baker v. Columbus Municipal Separate School District (1972), the District Court held that the National Teachers Examination "does not predict classroom effectiveness [of teachers, but also] does not even test for the great majority of factors that defendants believe are important in good teaching."[35] Similar statements of dictum have been expressed by other courts (e.g., Bridgeport Guardians, Inc. v. Members of the Bridgeport Civil Service Commission, 1973; Fowler v. Schwarzwalder, 1972).

In conclusion, the courts have demanded that, at a minimum, tests purportedly measuring an individual's cognitive, affective, or physical attributes must be able to adequately predict these attributes in relation to specific worker functions and activities. Therefore, it is reasonable to assume that judicial decisions based on Section 504, Subpart B employment practices regulation will follow the general movement toward requiring employers to validate testing instruments for qualified minority and handicapped individuals.

Delineation of Specific Regulatory Requirements[36]

There are four general requirements of Section 504, Subpart B regulation concerning employment practices. These general requirements are:
- No qualified handicapped person shall, on the basis of handicap, be subjected to discrimination in employment under any program or activity receiving Federal financial assistance;
- A recipient that receives assistance under the Education of the Handicapped Act shall take positive steps to employ and advance in employment qualified handicapped persons in programs assisted under that Act;
- A recipient shall make all decisions concerning employment under any program or activity in a manner which ensures that discrimination on the basis of handicap does not occur and may not limit, segregate, or classify applicants or employees in any way that adversely affects their opportunities or status because of handicap; and
- A recipient may not participate in a contractual or other relationship that has the effect of subjecting qualified handicapped applicants or employees to discrimination. These relationships include those pertaining to: (a) employment and referral agencies, (b) labor unions, (c) organizations providing or administering fringe benefits to employees, and (d) organizations providing training and apprenticeship programs.

Furthermore, a recipient's obligation to comply with these general requirements is not affected by any inconsistent term of any collective bargaining agreement to which it is a party.

Specifically, the four general requirements apply to the following substantive issues:
- The recruitment, advertising, and processing of applications for employment;
- The hiring, upgrading, promotion, award of tenure, demotion, transfer, layoff, termination, right to return from layoff, and rehiring;
- Rates of pay or any other form of compensation and changes in compensation;
- Job assignments, job classification, organizational structures, position descriptions, lines of progression, and seniority lists;
- Leaves of absence, sick leave, or any other leave;
- Fringe benefits available by virtue of employment, whether or not administered by the recipient;
- Selection and financial support for training, including apprenticeships, professional meetings, conferences, and other related activities, and selection for leaves of absence to pursue training;
- Employer sponsored activities, including social or recreational programs; and
- Any other term, condition, or privilege of employment.

In addition to the four general requirements of Section 504, Subpart B employment practices regulation, and the substantive issue areas which these general requirements apply, the Department of Health, Education and Welfare further stipulates regulation relative to reasonable accommodation, employment criteria, and preemployment inquiries.

Reasonable accommodation

Paragraph 84.12 of the regulation specifies that a recipient of Federal financial assistance must make reasonable accommodation to the known physical or mental limitations of an otherwise qualified handicapped applicant or employee unless the recipient can demonstrate that the accommodation would impose an undue hardship on the operation of its program. Reasonable accommodation may include:
- Making facilities used by employees readily accessible to and usable by handicapped persons; and
- Job restructuring, part-time or modified work schedules, acquisition or modification of equipment or devices, the provision of readers or interpreters, and other similar actions.

In determining whether an accommodation would impose an undue hardship on the operation of a recipient's program, factors to be considered include:
- The overall size of the recipient's program with respect to number of employees, number and type of facilities, and size of budget;

- The type of the recipient's operation, including the composition and structure of the recipient's workforce; and
- The nature and cost of the accommodation needed.

Employment criteria

In concert with the guidelines on employee selection procedures developed by the Equal Employment Opportunity Commission (Title 29, Chapter XIV, Section 1607 of the Code of Federal Regulations), the Department of Health, Education and Welfare requires that a recipient of any Federal financial assistance may not make use of any employment test or other selection criterion that screens out or tends to screen out handicapped persons or any class of handicapped persons unless:
- The test score or other selection criterion is shown to be job-related for the position in question; and
- Alternative job-related tests or criteria that do not screen out or tend to screen out as many handicapped persons are not shown by the Director of the Office for Civil Rights.

Furthermore, a recipient must select and administer tests concerning employment so as best to ensure that, when administered to an applicant or employee who has a handicap that impairs sensory, manual, or speaking skills, the test results accurately reflect the applicant's or employee's job skills, aptitude, or whatever other factor the test purports to measure, rather than reflecting the applicant's/employee's impaired sensory, manual, or speaking skills (except where those skills are the factors that the test purports to measure).

As stated previously, Section 713 (Title VII) of the Civil Rights Act of 1964 requires that employers, labor unions, and employment agencies that utilize testing procedures must ensure that such testing procedures are not designed or intended, in either administration or interpretation, to discriminate because of race, color, religion, sex or national origin. Although not stated explicitly, in effect, Section 504, Subpart B regulation extends Section 713 of the 1964 Civil Rights Act to include the handicapped. Furthermore, since the Equal Employment Opportunity Commission's *Guidelines on Employee Selection*[37] were developed to provide a "workable set of standards" for employers, unions, and employment agencies in conforming with the obligations of the Civil Rights Act, these same guidelines, although not obligatory, can be used by all recipients of Department of Health, Education and Welfare financial assistance (including public school systems) in conforming with the obligations of Section 504 of the Rehabilitation Act.

The Equal Employment Opportunity Commission's (EEOC) Guidelines on Employee Selection Procedures were developed:
- Based on the belief that properly validated and standardized selection procedures can significantly contribute to the implementation of nondiscriminatory personnel policies and when used in conjunction with

other tools of personnel assessment and complemented by programs of job design, may significantly aid in the development and maintenance of an efficient work force;
- Recognizing that there has been an increase in test usage and a concomitant increase in inappropriate testing practices; and
- To provide a set of testing procedure guidelines that are efficient and effective relative with managerial decision-making in the hiring, transfering, promoting, training, referral or retention of minority applicants and employees.

The term "test" is defined to include measure of:
- General intelligence;
- Mental ability;
- Learning ability;
- Specific intellectual abilities;
- Mechanical and clerical aptitudes;
- Dexterity and coordination;
- Knowledge and proficiency;
- Occupation; and
- Attitudes, personality or temperament.

The term "test" also includes all formal, scored, quantified or standardized techniques of assessing job suitability including:
- Specific qualifying or disqualifying personal history or background requirements;
- Specific educational or work history requirements;
- Scored interviews;
- Biographical information blanks;
- Interviewer's rating scales; and
- Scored application forms.

While the term "test" is used in the *Guidelines,* the EEOC regulation pertains to all employee selection procedures, including unscored or casual interviews and unscored application forms. Where there are data suggesting employment discrimination, an organization, including a school system, may be called upon to present evidence concerning the validity of unscored procedures as well as any test which may be used.

Paragraph 1607.3 of the EEOC *Guidelines* defines test discrimination as the use of any test which adversely affects hiring, promotion, transfer or any other employment or membership opportunity of classes protected by Title VII unless: (a) the test has been validated and evidences a high degree of utility, and (b) the person giving or acting upon the results of the particular test can demonstrate that alternative suitable hiring, transfer or promotion procedures are unavailable for his use. As paragraph 1607.3 implies, the substantive issue concerning test discrimination involves test validity.

In essence, validity can be "defined as the extent to which a testing procedure actually accomplishes what it seeks to accomplish or measures what it seeks to measure." More specific to the EEOC *Guidelines* and Section 504, Subpart B regulation, any test used as a basis for employment decisions must provide evidence that such tests are valid predictors of employee job performance. Without validity, the *presumed* relationships between test performance and job behavior may adversely affect minority or handicapped applicants who, in fact, may have the necessary qualifications for successful work performance. For this reason, the Equal Employment Opportunity Commission mandates that under no circumstances will the general reputation of a test, its author or its publisher, or casual reports of test utility be accepted in lieu of empirically validated studies. Declared specifically inappropriate are: (a) assumptions of validity based on test names or descriptive labels, (b) all forms of promotional literature, (c) data bearing on the frequency of a test's usage, (d) testimonial statements of sellers, users, or consultants, and (e) any other nonempirical or anecdotal accounts of testing practices or testing outcomes.

Paragraph 1607.4 of the EEOC *Guidelines* stipulates that each person using tests to select from among candidates for a position or from membership must have available for inspection evidence that the tests are being used in a nondiscriminatory manner. Evidence of validity should include:

- Where technically feasible, a test should be validated for each minority group with which it is used; therefore, any differential rejection rates that may exist, based on a test, must be relevant to performance on the jobs in question;
- Technical feasibility involves having or obtaining a sufficient number of minority individuals to achieve: (a) findings of statistical and practical significance, and (b) unbiased job performance criteria. Furthermore, it is the responsibility of the person claiming absence of technical feasibility to positively demonstrate evidence of this absence;
- Empirical data demonstrating that the test is predictive or significantly correlated with important elements of work behavior which comprise or are relevant to the job for which a candidate is being evaluated;
- In predicting worker behavior, if job progression structures and seniority provisions are to established that new employees will probably, within a reasonable period of time and in the "great majority" of cases, progress to a higher level, it may be considered that candidate work behavior is being evaluated for jobs at that higher level. However, where job progression is not so nearly automatic, or the time span is such that higher level jobs or employees' potential may be expected to change in significant ways, candidate work behavior should be evaluated for a job at or near the entry level; and
- Where a test is to be used in different units of a multiunit organization and no significant differences exist between units, jobs, and applicant populations, evidence obtained in one unit may suffice for the others. Similarly, where the validation process requires the collection of data throughout a multiunit organization, evidence of validity specific to each unit may not be required.

Delineated in paragraph 1607.5 of the EEOC Guidelines are the minimum standards required for validation. In general, empirical evidence in support of a test's validity must be based on studies employing accepted procedures for determining criterion-related validity. Criterion-related validity, sometimes referred to as concurrent validity or predictive validity, asks the question: Does the test compare well with external variables (e.g., job related worker performance) considered to be direct measure of the characteristic of behavior in question? If criterion-related validity is not reasonable, then evidence of content or construct validity is sufficient. Content validity asks the question: How well does the content of the test sample the kinds of things about which conclusions are to be drawn? Construct validity asks the question: To what extent do certain explanatory concepts or qualities account for performance on the test? However, evidence for content or construct validity should be accompanied by sufficient information from job analyses to demonstrate the relevance of the content (in the case of job knowledge or proficiency tests) or the construct (in the case of trait measures). Evidence of content validity alone may be acceptable for well-developed tests that consist of suitable samples of essential knowledge, skills or behaviors composing the job in question. The types of knowledge, skills or behaviors do not include those which can be acquired in a brief orientation to the job.

Although the Equal Employment Opportunity Commission stipulates that any appropriate validation strategy may be used to develop evidence of validity, the following minimum standards must be met:

- Where a validity study is conducted in which tests are administered to applicants, with criterion data collected later, the sample of subjects must be representative of the normal or typical candidate group for the job or jobs in question;
- The applicant sample should also be representative of the minority population available for the job or jobs in question in the local labor market;
- Where a validity study is conducted in which tests are administered to present employees, the sample must be representative of the minority groups currently included in the applicant population;
- If it is not technically feasible to include minority employees in validation studies conducted on the present work force, the conduct of validation study without minority candidates does not relieve any person or organization of the obligation for validation when inclusion of minority candidates become technically feasible;
- Tests must be administered and scored under controlled and standardized conditions, with proper safeguards to protect the security of test scores and to ensure that scores do not enter into any judgments of employee adequacy that are to be used as criterion measures;
- Copies of tests and test manuals, including instructions for administration, scoring, and interpretation of test results, that are privately developed and/or are not available through normal commercial channels, must be included as a part of the validation evidence;
- The work behaviors or other criteria of employee adequacy which the test is intended to predict or identify must be fully described and, in the case of rating techniques, the appraisal form(s) and instructions to the rater(s) must be included as a part of the validation evidence;

- Whatever criteria used must represent major or critical work behaviors as revealed by careful job analysis;
- With the possibility of bias inherent in subjective evaluations, supervisory rating techniques must be carefully developed, and the ratings need to be closely examined for evidence of bias;
- Data must be generated and results separately reported for minority and nonminority groups wherever technically feasible;
- Where a minority group is sufficiently large to constitute an identifiable factor in the local labor market, but validation data have not been developed and presented separately for that group, evidence of satisfactory validity based on other groups will be regarded as only provisional compliance pending separate validation of the test for the minority group in question;
- A test which is differentially valid may not be used with those in which it is not valid; and
- Where a test is valid for two groups but one group characteristically obtains higher test scores than the other without a corresponding difference in job performance, cutoff scores must be set so as to predict the same probability of job success in both groups.

In assessing the utility of a test, the Equal Employment Opportunity Commission stipulates that the following considerations are applicable:

- The relationship between the test and at least one relevant criterion must be statistically significant at the .05, or higher, level;
- The use of a single test as the sole selection device should be scrutinized closely when that test is valid against only one component of job performance;
- In addition to statistical significance, the relationship between the test and criterion should have practical significance. The magnitude of the relationship needed for practical significance or usefullness is affected by several factors, including: (a) the larger the proportion of applicants who are hired for or placed on the job, the higher the relationship needs to be, (b) the larger the proportion of applicants who become satisfactory employees when not selected on the basis of the test, the higher the relationship needs to be, and (c) the smaller the economic and human risks involved in hiring an unqualified applicant relative to the rights entailed in rejecting a qualified applicant, the greater the relationship needs to be.

Delineated in paragraph 1607.6 of the EEOC *Guidelines* are the requirements for presenting the results of a validation study. These requirements include:

- Graphical and statistical representations of the relationships between the test and the criteria;
- Average scores for all tests and criteria for all relevant subgroups, including minority and nonminority groups where differential validation is required;
- Whenever statistical adjustments are made in validity results for less than perfect reliability or for restriction of score range in the test or the criterion, or both, the supporting evidence from the validation study must be presented in detail;

- For each test that is to be established or continued as an organizational employee selection instrument, the minimum acceptable cutoff (passing) score on the test must be reported; and
- Each operational cutoff score should be reasonable and consistent with normal expectations or proficiency within the work force or group on which the study was conducted.

In cases where the validity of a test cannot be determined (e.g., the number of subjects is less than that required for statistical computation, or an appropriate criterion measure cannot be developed), evidence from validity studies conducted in other organizations, such as that reported in test manuals and professional literature, may be considered acceptable when: (a) the studies pertain to jobs which are comparable (i.e., have basically the same task elements), and (b) there are no major differences in contextual variables or sample composition which are likely to significantly affect validity. Demonstrable evidence of job comparability and the absence of contextual variables or sample differences must be presented by any organization utilizing validity studies conducted in other situations. An organization may continue to use a test without the required evidence of validity if determination of criterion-related validity in a specific setting is impracticable. However, continued use of the test necessitates: (a) some evidence of validity having been determined (as described above), or (b) validation procedures have been initiated and will be completed within a reasonable period of time. Furthermore, an organization may have to alter or suspend test cutoff scores so that score ranges broad enough to permit the identification of criterion-related validity will be obtained.

The Equal Employment Opportunity Commission also stipulates that even though a test or other employee selection standard is validated against job performance in accordance with the EEOC Guidelines, standards not applied to other applicants or employees cannot be imposed upon those individuals protected by Title VII. It can be reasonably assumed that this restriction is also applicable to handicapped individuals. Also, employers, unions, and employment agencies should provide an opportunity for retesting and reconsideration to "failure" candidates who have availed themselves of more training or experience.

It should be pointed out that neither the EEOC Guidelines on employee selection nor Section 504, Subpart B regulation discuss what is considered the basic attribute which every employment test or procedure must possess—reliability. "By reliability we mean the accuracy of the data in the sense of their stability, repeatability, or precision."[38] This omission is inconsequential. As Fox states,

> There is a one-way relationship between reliability and validity. Reliability for a procedure is essential before its validity can be considered, and the actual reliability sets the ceiling for the maximum validity [an] instrument can possess.[39]

High validity ensures high reliability. By requiring employment selection procedures to be adequately validated, the EEOC Guidelines ensure that appropriate reliability is achieved.

Preemployment inquires

Paragraph 84.14 of Section 504, Subpart B regulation specifies that when a recipient of Federal financial assistance is taking (a) remedial action to correct the effects of past discrimination, (b) voluntary action to overcome the effects of conditions that resulted in limited participation by handicapped individuals in a recipient's programs or activities, or (c) taking affirmative action pursuant to Section 503 of the Act, the recipient may request applicants for employment to indicate whether and to what extent they are handicapped provided that:

- The recipient states clearly on any written questionnaire or makes clear orally if no written questionnaire is used that the information requested is intended for use solely in connection with remedial, voluntary, or affirmative action efforts; and
- The recipient states clearly that (a) the information is being requested on a voluntary basis, (b) that it will be kept confidential, (c) that refusal to provide such information will not subject the applicant or employee to any adverse treatment, and (d) that such information will be used only in accordance with the stipulation of paragraph 84.14 of the regulation.

Paragraph 84.14 does not prohibit a recipient of Federal financial assistance from conditioning an offer of employment on the results of a medical examination conducted prior to the employee's assumption of duties. Two impositions, however, have been placed on this condition of employment:

- All entering employees are subjected to such an examination regardless of handicap; and
- The results of such an examination are used only in accordance with the appropriate remedial, voluntary, or affirmative action efforts.

Information relative to the medical condition or history of the applicant must be collected and maintained on separate employment forms and must be accorded the same confidentiality as medical records. This medical information may be utilized so that:

- Supervisors and managers are informed regarding restrictions on the work or duties of handicapped persons and regarding necessary accommodations;
- First aid and safety personnel are informed, when appropriate, if the condition might require emergency treatment; and
- Government officials investigating compliance with Section 504 regulation shall be provided relevant information upon request.

To understand the statutory and regulatory requirements of Section 504, Subpart B relative to the various dimensions of local educational agency administrative responsibilities, the above employment practices requirements need to be placed within the context of a general discussion of staffing issues.

Staffing Issues Relative to the Structure and Operation of Local Educational Agencies

Section 504, Subpart B regulation does *not* require local educational agencies to develop and implement affirmative action programs. However, three types of organizational action are required in lieu of an affirmative action program. These action are: (a) remedial action, (b) voluntary action, and (c) self-evaluation. If the Director of the Office for Civil Rights finds that a local educational agency has discriminated against individuals on the basis of handicap in violation of Section 504, the local educational agency must take such remedial action as the Director deems necessary to overcome the effects of the discrimination. The Director may require remedial action (a) with respect to handicapped persons who are no longer participants in the district's program but who were participants in the program when discrimination occurred, or (b) with respect to handicapped persons who would have been participants in the program had the discrimination not occurred.

A local educational agency may take voluntary action, in addition to any remedial action that is required, to overcome the effects of conditions that resulted in limited practicpation by qualified handicapped individuals in the local district's program or activity.

A developing national sensitivity to the employment problems confronted by individuals with handicaps virtually mandates that local educational agencies lead the way in taking "positive steps" in addressing and remediating these employment problems. It is essential that districts develop a specific self-evaluation design, which consists of the self-evaluation plan, and district policies and procedures for its implementation. This self-evaluation program should include input from all levels of the district during both the planning and implementation phases. Specified in paragraph 87.4 of the regulation are the following self-evaluation requirements:

- Within one year of the effective date of publishing Section 504 regulation (May 4, 1977), local school districts must: (a) evaluate, with the assistance of handicapped individuals and organizations, current district policies and practices that do not meet Section 504 requirements, (b) modify such district policies and practices, and (c) take appropriate remedial steps to eliminate the effects of any discrimination that resulted from adherence to such policies and practices; and
- A local school district that employs fifteen or more persons must, for at least three years following completion of the self-evaluation, maintain on file and make available for public inspection: (a) a list of the interested individual's consulted, (b) a description of areas examined and any problems identified, and (c) a description of any modifications made and of any remedial steps taken.

Schematically presented in Figure 1 are the necessary conceptual components for planning, conducting, and analyzing a self-evaluation design.

Figure 1
Conceptual Components for a Self-Evaluation Design

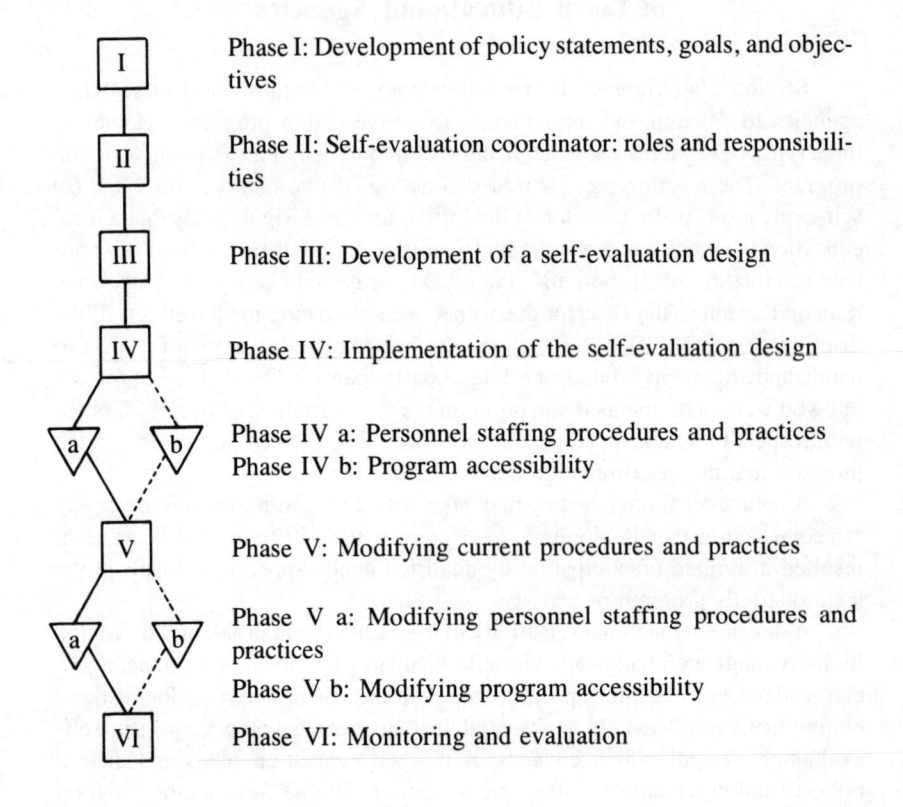

I	Phase I: Development of policy statements, goals, and objectives
II	Phase II: Self-evaluation coordinator: roles and responsibilities
III	Phase III: Development of a self-evaluation design
IV	Phase IV: Implementation of the self-evaluation design
a b	Phase IV a: Personnel staffing procedures and practices Phase IV b: Program accessibility
V	Phase V: Modifying current procedures and practices
a b	Phase V a: Modifying personnel staffing procedures and practices Phase V b: Modifying program accessibility
VI	Phase VI: Monitoring and evaluation

In the remaining portion of Chapter II, we will examine those self-evaluation conceptual components applicable to a local educational agencies employment practices. These conceptual components are:
- Phase I: Development of policy statements, goals, and objectives concerning the self-evaluation design;
- Phase II: Self-evaluation coordinator: roles and responsibilities;
- Phase III: Development of a self-evaluation design;
- Phase IV: Implementation of the self-evaluation design, including an analysis of current personnel staffing procedures through the use of job and organizational analysis.
- Phase V: Modify current personnel staffing procedures, including (a) modification of physical accessibility barriers, (b) specific job-related accommodations, (c) modification of examination procedures for employment, and (d) development of alternative employment procedures;
- Phase VI: Monitoring and evaluation.

Phase I: Development of policy statements, goals, and objectives concerning the self-evaluation design

The first phase of the self-evaluation design requires the local educational agency's school board and superintendent to: (a) define district goals in accordance with complying with Section 504, Subpart B regulation, (b) identify performance indicators and standards for goals, (c) set division/department objectives consistent with goals, and (d) delineate district goals, performance indicators/standards and division/department objectives in a written policy statement document. Furthermore, the school board and superintendent will have to delegate the responsibility of planning for and conducting the self-evaluation to an individual—the self-evaluation coordinator. This individual must have: (a) knowledge concerning Federal statutory and regulatory requirements, (b) knowledge concerning state statutory and regulatory requirements, (c) knowledge of state and local administrative responses to Federal statutory and regulatory requirements, (d) a capability of working with all levels of personnel within the local educational agency, (e) authority and knowledge to plan, conduct, and analyze a job analysis study (i.e., job analysis profile and narrative report), (f) authority and knowledge to plan, conduct, and analyze an architectural barriers discrepancy analysis, and (g) authority to make recommendations for program modifications and accommodations. In general, these criteria eliminate employing external third party personnel to conduct the self-evaluation. After delegating the responsibility of conducting the self-evaluation to an individual, the school board and superintendent also need to: (a) allocate specific resources (e.g., fiscal, material, and personnel) to be used for planning the self-evaluation, (b) be willing to negotiate for additional fiscal, material and personnel resources to be used for conducting the self-evaluation, (c) delineate the specific social and political restrictions placed upon the self-evaluation coordinator and his/her staff, and (d) be willing to objectively review and act upon recommendations and suggestions provided by all interested individuals and groups.

Phase II: Self-evaluation coordinator— roles and responsibilities

The salient question that the self-evaluation coordinator must address is: What is the nature of the relationship between that individual who assesses a local educational agency's compliance with Section 504, Subpart B employment practices regulation, and those individuals responsible for planning, designing, and developing program materials, personnel, and performance specification. This question has been examined by several professional "research and development" specialists, and they have concluded, "Both from an evaluation and a development perspective, [there has] emerged . . . a picture of the developer and evaluator not as distinct functions but rather as a continuum which has at one pole a pure developer who may not interact with an evaluator and at the other pole a pure evaluator who performs his duties in isolation from a developer."[40] As Borich has noted, "by identifying subsurface tasks and activities which demarcate the space between pure development and evaluation we can begin to link the developer to the evaluator with a logical sequence of real-life responsibilities."[41] Delineated in Figure 2 is the demarcation between pure development and evaluation.

Figure 2[42]
Demarcation Between Pure Development and Evaluation

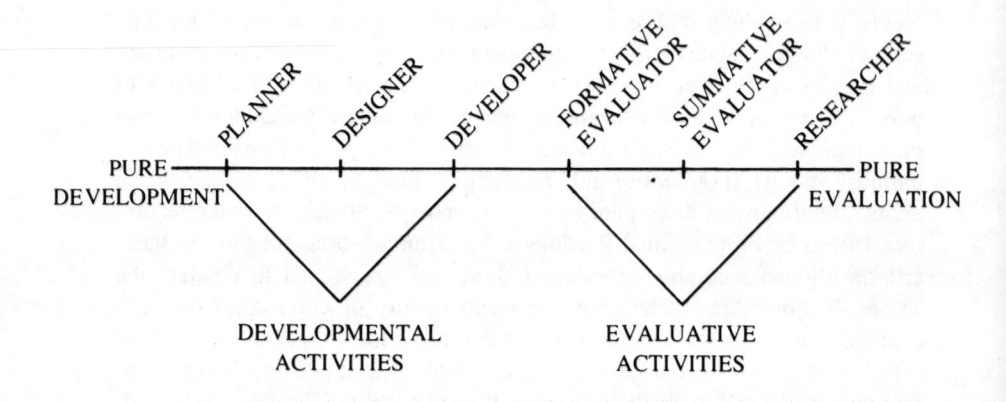

```
                    PLANNER  DESIGNER  DEVELOPER  FORMATIVE   SUMMATIVE   RESEARCHER
                                                  EVALUATOR   EVALUATOR
PURE ──────┼─────────┼─────────┼─────────┼─────────┼─────────┼────── PURE
DEVELOPMENT                                                          EVALUATION
            \        |        /         \         |         /
             \       |       /           \        |        /
              \      |      /             \       |       /
               \_____|_____/               _____|_____/
              DEVELOPMENTAL                   EVALUATIVE
               ACTIVITIES                     ACTIVITIES
```

The six development/evaluation "real-life responsibilities" are defined as:

- Planner: organizes and marshal materials and personnel for the development task (e.g., modifications in current employment procedures and practices);
- Designer: writes content and performance specifications for the program or product;
- Developer: constructs product or program that meets content and performance specifications;
- Formative evaluator: assesses product or program components for the purpose of revision and modification;
- Summative evaluator: assesses product or program in toto for the purpose of adoption or continuation; and
- Researcher: formulates and tests hypotheses concerning the program or product vis a vis theoretical framework.[43]

For most local educational agencies, the developmental activities will be the responsibility of the school board, superintendent, and appropriate administrative staff (e.g., assistant superintendents or program directors), while the evaluative activities will usually be the responsibility of the self-evaluation coordinator. In examining this issue, Borich has concluded,

> As we move toward the center of the continuum, we identify those activities for which the evaluator and developer are likely to have the strongest interrelationship. It is at this point that role functions may change, the developer performing some of the evaluation and the evaluator performing some of the development.
>
> It is at this intersection also that a major question arises and perhaps the most controversy exists: should the evaluator be distinct from the developers or can these roles represent responsibilities of a single individual? For the answer to this question we must look to the contexts in which these two arrangements have been used to determine the extent to which the product or program has profited from each. In doing so, on the one hand, we are warned that when role distinctions become unclear the program may suffer from what has come to be called co-option. This refers to the situation in which the evaluator becomes so immersed in the values and feelings of the developers that evaluation is no longer an objective guide to program or product development. And, on the other hand, we are warned that development is so closely tied to formative evaluation that any separation of roles is at best an artificial distinction that may detract from rather than add to the development process. The truth of either claim is not well documented.[44]

Little has been said about the role functions of the planners/designers/developers and formative/summative/research evaluator. Activities of the former lead to, and activities of the latter result from, the kind of interrelationship that takes place between each group. "It is not uncommon . . . for a [self-evaluation] program . . . to be planned and designed in such a way as to either encourage or preclude a certain kind of relationship between . . . developer and [the] self-evaluator, or that once this relationship has taken place, the . . . self-evaluator is forced to accept regardless of its effect upon the quality" of the district's employment procedures and practices.[45]

Scriven has provided one answer to the problems of exchanging role functions for the school system's developers and the self-evaluation coordinator. Scriven has called his approach goal-free evaluation.

> The goal-free evaluation role is one in which a evaluator views program development and evaluation from a perspective more general than any activity and hopefully from a perspective that includes all activities, so that planning, designing, developing, and formative and summative evaluation may be seen at points in time by a single individual. Co-option may become much more apparent from such a broad perspective than when only the interrelationship between . . . evaluator and developer is focused upon. A narrow focus can neither provide data as to why the co-option occurred or what its effects may be at later role functions in the continuum. Therefore, a goal-free evaluator may in some respects perform the role of meta-evaluator inasmuch as he is not tied to a specific role function. Goal-free evaluators . . . may well encourage any kind of relationship between . . . evaluator and developers that seems profitable.[46]

Finally, Borich offers two important suggestions concerning the role of the self-evaluator. First, no one relationship may be appropriate across all self-evaluation projects and, second, the nature of the relationship between self-evaluator and school system decision-makers and program developers might better depend upon the nature of the individuals involved and the kind of school system being evaluated. Assuming that the self-evaluation coordinator is sensitive to the nature of his relationship with school system decision-makers and program developers, one might argue for a laissez faire perspective as to the precise role of the self-evaluation coordinator and the school system decision-makers and program developers.

Phase III: Development of a self-evaluation design

The self-evaluation coordinator and his staff must be able to address six decision-making dimensions. These six decision-making dimensions are: (a) focusing the self-evaluation, (b) collection of information, (c) organization of information, (d) analysis of information, (e) reporting of self-evaluation information, and (f) administration of the self-evaluation project. Delineated in Figure 3 are the six decision-making dimensions and specific decision-making points applicable to each dimension. Figure 3 is an attempt to provide a general list of decision-making dimensions appropriate for a variety of local educational agency self-evaluation designs. By presenting this general list, the author is in agreement with Stufflebeam in asserting that "the logical structure of evaluation design is the same for all types of evaluation." Presented below is a paraphrased and slightly modified excerpt from an address delivered by Daniel Stufflebeam at Sarasota, Florida, January 19, 1969. This excerpt is included in Worthen and Sander's *Educational Evaluation: Theory and Practice*,[47] and is applicable for addressing the salient decision-making activities the self-evaluation coordinator and his staff will be involved.

> Once the self-evaluation coordinator has selected an evaluation strategy, he must next select or develop a design to implement his evaluation. This is a difficult task since few generalized evaluation designs exist which are adequate to meet emergent needs for evaluation. Thus, the self-evaluation coordinator must typically develop evaluation designs de novo. However, in an attempt to provide a general guide for developing self-evaluation designs, the author will attempt to define design in general terms and to explicate the general structure of designs for educational self-evaluation. Hopefully, this general treatment of self-evaluation design will be some help to self-evaluation coordinators in ordering their minds as they approach problems of designing self-evaluations.
>
> *Design Defined.* In general, design is the preparation of a set of decision situations for implementation toward the achievement of specified objectives. This definition says three things. First, one must identify the objectives to be achieved through implementation of the design. Second, this definition says that one should identify and define the decision situations in the procedure for achieving the self-evaluation objective. Third, for each identified decision situation the evaluator needs to make a choice among the available alternatives. Thus, the completed self-

Figure 3[48]

The logical structure of evaluation design is the same for all types of evaluation, whether context, input, process or product evaluation. The parts, briefly, are as follows:

A. *Focusing the Evaluation*
   1. Identify the major level(s) of decision-making to be served, e.g., local, state, or national.
   2. For each level of decision-making, project the decision situations to be served and describe each one in terms of its locus, focus, criticality, timing, and composition of alternatives.
   3. Define criteria for each decision situation by specifying variables for measurement and standards for use in the judgment of alternatives.
   4. Define policies within which the evaluator must operate.

B. *Collection of Information*
   1. Specify the source of the information to be collected.
   2. Specify the instruments and methods for collecting the needed information.
   3. Specify the sampling procedure to be employed.
   4. Specify the conditions and schedule for information collection.

C. *Organization of Information*
   1. Provide a format for the information which is to be collected.
   2. Designate a means for performing the analysis.

D. *Analysis of Information*
   1. Select the analytical procedures to be employed.
   2. Designate a means for performing the analysis.

E. *Reporting of Information*
   1. Define the audiences for the evaluation reports.
   2. Specify means for providing information to the audiences
   3. Specify the format for evaluation reports and/or reporting sessions.
   4. Schedule the reporting of information.

F. *Administration of the Evaluation*
   1. Summarize the evaluation schedule.
   2. Define staff and resource requirements and plans for meeting these requirements.
   3. Specify means for meeting policy requirements for conduct of the evaluation.
   4. Evaluate the potential of the evaluation design for providing information which is valid, reliable, credible, timely, and pervasive.
   5. Specify and schedule means for periodic updating of the evaluation design.
   6. Provide a budget for the total evaluation program.

evaluation design would contain a set of decisions as to how the self-evaluation is to be conducted and what instruments will be used.

It should be useful to self-evaluation coordinators to have available a list of the decision situations which are common to many self-evaluation designs. This would enable them to approach problems of self-evaluation design in a systematic manner. Further, such a list could serve as an outline for the content of self-evaluation sections in research and development proposals. Funding agencies could also find such a list useful in structuring their general guidelines for self-evaluations. Also, such a list should be useful to training institutions for defining the role of the self-evaluation specialist.

Figure 3 is an attempt to provide such a general list of decision situations for self-evaluation designs. By presenting this general list we are asserting that the structure of self-evaluation design is the same for all local educational agency self-evaluations. This structure includes six major parts. These are (a) focusing the self-evaluation, (b) information collection, (c) information organization, (d) information analysis, (e) information reporting, and (f) the administration of self-evaluation projects. Each of these parts will be considered separately.

Focusing the Self-Evaluation. The first part of the structure of self-evaluation design is that of focusing the self-evaluation. The purpose of this part is to spell out the ends for the self-evaluation and to define policies within which the self-evaluation must be conducted. Specifically this part of self-evaluation design includes four steps.

The first step is to identify the major levels of decision-making for which self-evaluation information must be provided. For example, Section 504 self-evaluative information from local schools is needed at local, state and national levels. It is important to take all relevant levels into account in the design of self-evaluations since different levels may have different information requirements and since the different Federal, state and local agencies may need information at different times.

Having identified the major levels of decision-making to be served by self-evaluation, the next step is to identify and define the decision situations to be served at each level. Given our present low state of knowledge about decision-making in education, this is a very difficult task. However, it is also a very important one and should be done as well as is practicable. First, decision situations should be identified in terms of those responsible for making the decisions, e.g., school board members, the superintendent, principals, etc. Next, major types of decision situations should be identified, e.g., appropriational, allocational, approval, or continuation. Then these types of decision situations should be classified by focus, e.g., research, development, diffusion or adoption in the case of instrumental outcomes, or knowledge or understanding in the case of consequential outcomes. (This step is especially helpful toward identifying relevant evaluative criteria.) These identified decision situations should then be analyzed in terms of their relative criticality. In this way relatively less important decisions which would expend self-evaluation resources needlessly can be eliminated from further consideration. Next, the timing of the decision situation to be served should be estimated so that the self-evaluation can be geared to provide relevant data prior to the time when decisions must be made. And, finally, an attempt should be made to explicate each important decision situation in terms of the alternatives which may reasonably be considered in reaching the decision.

Once the decision situations to be served have been explicated, the next step is to define relevant information requirements. Specifically, the self-evaluation coordinator should define criteria for each decision situation by specifying variables for measurement and standards for use in the judgment of alternatives.

The final step in focusing the self-evaluation is to define policies within which the coordinator must operate. Also, it is necessary to determine who will receive self-evaluation reports and who will have access to them. Finally, it is necessary to define the limits of access to data for the self-evaluation staff.

Collection of Information. The second major part of the structure of self-evaluation design is that of planning the collection of information. This section must obviously be keyed very closely to the criteria which were identifed in the evaluation focus part of the design.

Using those criteria, the self-evaluation coordinator should first identify the sources of the information to be collected. These information sources should be defined in two respects: first, the origins for the information, e.g., teachers or principals, and second, the present state of the information, i.e., in recorded or non-recorded form.

Next, one should specify instruments and methods for collecting the needed information. Examples include job analysis studies, observation, questioning (including interview schedules), and narrative reports. Michael and Metfessel have provided a comprehensive list of instruments with potential relevance for data collection in self-evaluations.

For each instrument that is to be administered, one should next specify the sampling procedure to be employed. Where possible, one should avoid administering too many instruments to the same person. Thus, sampling without replacement across instruments can be a useful technique.

Finally, one should develop a master schedule for the collection of information. This schedule should detail the interrelations between samples, instruments, and dates for the collection of information.

Organization of Information. A frequent disclaimer in self-evaluation reports is that resources were inadequate to allow for processing all of the pertinent data. If this problem is not to arise, one should make definite plans regarding the third part of self-evaluation design: organization of information. Organizing the information that is to be collected includes providing a format for classifying information and designating means for coding, organizing, storing, and retrieving the information.

Analysis of Information. The fourth major part of self-evaluation design is analysis of information. The purpose of this part is to provide for the descriptive or statistical analyses of the information which is to be reported to decision-makers. This part also includes interpretations and recommendations. As with the organization of information it is important that the self-evaluation design specify means for performing the analyses. The role should be assigned specifically to a qualified member of the evaluation team or to an agency which specializes in doing data analyses. Also, it is important that those who will be responsible for the analysis of information participate in designing the analysis procedures.

Reporting of Information. The fifth part of self-evaluation design is the reporting of information. The purpose of this part of a design is to insure that the self-evaluation coordinator and administrative decision-makers will have timely access to the information they need and that they will receive it in a manner and form which facilitates their use of the information. In accordance with the policy for the self-evaluation, audiences for self-evaluation reports should be identified and defined. Then means should be defined for providing information to each audience. Subsequently, the format for self-evaluation reports and reporting sessions should be specified. And, finally, a master schedule of self-evaluation reporting should be provided. This schedule should define the interrelations between audiences, reports, and dates for reporting information.

Administration of Self-Evaluation Projects. The last part of self-evaluation design is that of administration of the self-evaluation. The purpose of this part is to provide an overall plan for executing the self-evaluation design. The first step is to define the overall self-evaluation schedule. For this purpose it often would be useful to employ a scheduling technique such as program evaluation and review techniques (PERT). The second step is to define staff requirements and plans for meeting these requirements. The third step is to specify means for meeting policy requirements for conduct of the self-evaluation. The fourth step is to evaluate the potential of the self-evaluation design for providing information which is valid, reliable, credible, timely, and pervasive. The fifth step is to specify and schedule means for periodic updating of the self-evaluation design. And, the sixth and final step is to provide a budget for the self-evaluation.

Phase IVa: Implementation of the self-evaluation design

To comply with Section 504, Subpart B employment practices requirements, the self-evaluation coordinator will need to delineate the: (a) discrepancy between current local educational agency employment practices/procedures, and Section 504, Subpart B regulation requirements, and (b) discrepancy between current physical accessibility to the districts facilities/work environment and applicable Section 504, Subparts B and C. And to successfully delinate the discrepancy between current employment practices/procedures and Section 504, Subpart B regulation requirements, the self-evaluation coordinator must understand the role of job and organizational analysis in the staffing process. The results of job and organizational analyses can be used to compare current employment practices/procedures (i.e., current performance) with the requirements of what should be (i.e., Section 504 standards). Schematically presented in Figure 4 are the necessary conceptual components for understanding the role of job and organizational analysis in the staffing process.

As indicated in Figure 4, there are six basic components of job and organizational analysis in the staffing process. These components are:
- Job analysis and design;
- Organizational structure and organizational structural analysis;

Figure 4

Conceptual Components for Understanding the Role of Job and Organizational Analysis in the Staffing Process

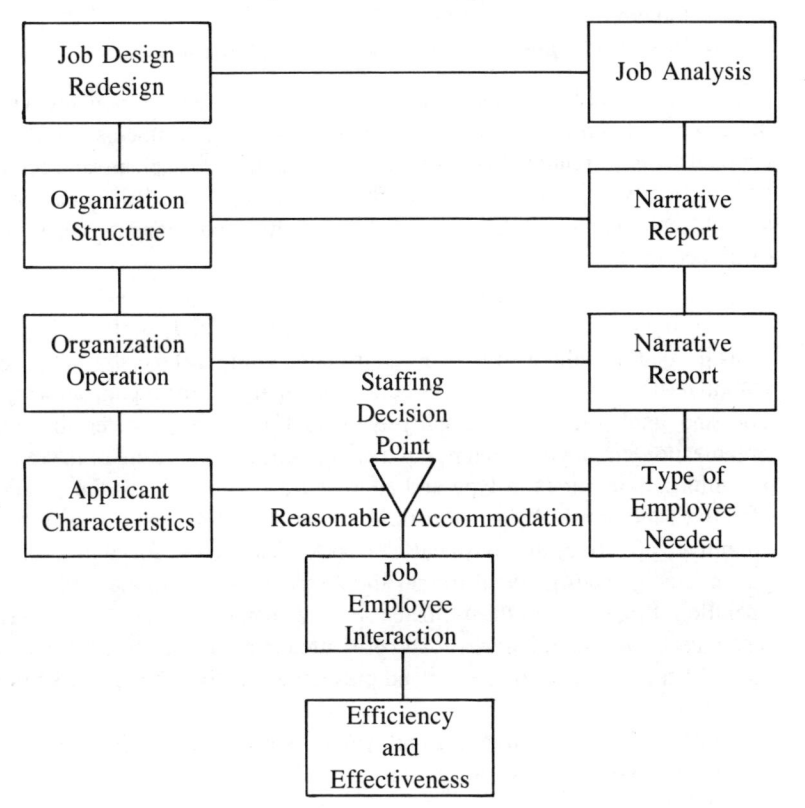

```
┌──────────────┐                           ┌──────────────┐
│  Job Design  │───────────────────────────│ Job Analysis │
│   Redesign   │                           │              │
└──────┬───────┘                           └──────┬───────┘
       │                                          │
┌──────┴───────┐                           ┌──────┴───────┐
│ Organization │───────────────────────────│   Narrative  │
│  Structure   │                           │    Report    │
└──────┬───────┘                           └──────┬───────┘
       │                                          │
┌──────┴───────┐                           ┌──────┴───────┐
│ Organization │          Staffing         │   Narrative  │
│  Operation   │          Decision         │    Report    │
└──────┬───────┘           Point           └──────┬───────┘
       │                     ▽                    │
┌──────┴───────┐                           ┌──────┴───────┐
│   Applicant  │                           │    Type of   │
│Characteristics──Reasonable  Accommodation│   Employee   │
│              │                           │    Needed    │
└──────────────┘                           └──────────────┘
                   ┌──────────────┐
                   │     Job      │
                   │   Employee   │
                   │  Interaction │
                   └──────┬───────┘
                          │
                   ┌──────┴───────┐
                   │  Efficiency  │
                   │     and      │
                   │ Effectiveness│
                   └──────────────┘
```

Defines and determines necessary (a) worker functions, (b) work methodologies and techniques, (c) machines, tools, equipment, and work aids, and (d) materials, products, subject matter, or services and (e) cognitive, affective, and physical traits required of the worker.

Defines and determines (a) type of formal organization, (b) type of informal organization, (c) authority characteristics, and (d) operation characteristics (e.g., planning/programming, control, and information systems).

Defines and determines (a) motivation and incentive characteristics, (b) organizational style and climate, (c) leadership/supervisory characteristics, (d) decision-making style, (e) communication networks, and (f) staffing process (e.g., manpower planning, recruitment procedures, and hiring procedures).

- Organizational operation and organizational operational analysis;
- Personnel decision points, including applicant characteristics and type of employee needed;
- Job/employee interaction; and
- Organization/employee efficiency and effectiveness.

Administrative planning concerning the first three components will require substantial managerial decision-making before adjustments in local educational agency organizational structure and operation take place, and certainly before effective "positive steps" can be taken to employ qualified handicapped school personnel. Therefore, each of these three components needs to be examined in detail.

Job analysis: What it is and its uses.[49] Job information is the basic data used by industry, government and private agencies, and employee organizations for making administrative decisions concerning: (a) the staffing process, (b) job design, (c) organization structure and analysis, (d) organization operation and analysis, (e) job/employee interaction, and (f) determination of organization/employee efficiency and effectiveness. The nature of the required job information varies in type and approach according to: (a) the cognitive, affective, and physical characteristics of an applicant for employment, (b) the cognitive, affective, and physical characteristics needed for appropriate job performance, and (c) type of formal and informal organizational structure and operation. Regardless of the ultimate use for which it is intended, however, the data must be accurate, inclusive, and presented in a form suitable for study and use. The technique for obtaining and presenting this information is known as "job analysis".

In the U.S. Training and Employment Service, job analysis involves a systematic study of the worker in terms of:
- What the worker does in relation to data, people, and things (e.g., worker functions);
- The methodologies and techniques employed (e.g., work fields);
- The machines, tools, equipment, and work aids used;
- The materials, products, subject matter, or services which results; and
- The traits required by the worker.

This section of the handbook is devoted to an explanation of the procedures and techniques that should be employed by local educational agencies to analyze jobs and to record the analyses. Although the procedures and techniques were developed with the occupational information needs of a variety of manpower programs in mind, they are applicable to any job analysis study, regardless of the intended utilization of the data. And as stated previously, the procedures and techniques described in this handbook are appropriate for all workers, regardless of the type of work involved or the unique cognitive, affective, or physical characteristics of any individual worker.

Job analyses are basic for supplying occupational information needed for manpower development and utilization programs in local educational agencies.

Some of the major areas of use are:
- Recruitment and placement: providing meaningful and correct job data for the recruitment and selection of workers;
- Better utilization of workers: determining job relationships useful in the transfer and promotion of workers to facilitate opening up job opportunities at the entry level. Also, determining actual physical demands of the job and suggesting job adjustments to facilitate improved utilization of handicapped workers;
- Job restructuring: restructuring jobs to make better use of the available work force, and to assist in opening entry job opportunities for the less than fully qualified, in facilitating the placement of workers in hard to fill jobs, and in providing trainee jobs;
- Training: determining training needs and developing training programs (e.g., in-service training programs). The content of the training curriculum, the amount of time required for training, and the basis for the selection of trainees are dependent, in part, upon knowledge of the jobs.
- Performance evaluation: providing an objective basis for developing performance standards; and
- Plant safety: improving building site safety through the disclosure of job hazards.

Concepts and principles in job analysis.[50] With respect to employment, Section 504, Subpart B regulation defines a qualified handicapped person as a handicapped person who, with reasonable accommodation, can perform the essential functions of the job in question. Reasonable accommodation may include:
- Making facilities used by employees readily accessible to and usable by handicapped persons; and
- Job restructuring, part-time or modified work schedules, acquisition or modification of equipment or devices, relocation of particular offices or jobs, the provision of readers or interpreters, and other similar actions.

Four additional employment concepts, not defined in Section 504 regulation, are necessary for understanding job analysis. Therefore, to eliminate possible confusion and to clarify terms, the U.S. Training and Employment Service has developed the following definitions for use in job analysis:
- Element: the smallest step into which it is practicable to subdivide any work activity without analyzing separate motions, movements, and mental processes involved. There are six broad categories of elements (i.e., worker function elements; data elements; people elements; machine, tool, equipment, and work aid elements; work field elements; and material, product, subject matter, and service elements);
- Task: one or more elements and is one of the distinct activities that constitute logical and necessary steps in the performance of a specific work activity by the worker. A task is created whenever human effort, physical or mental, is exerted to accomplish a specific purpose;
- Competency: a collection of tasks constituting a distinct set of related work activities;
- Position: a collection of competencies constituting the total work assignment of a single worker;

- Job: a group of positions which are identical with respect to their major or significant tasks and competencies and sufficiently alike to justify their being covered by a single analysis. There may be one or many persons employed in the same job.

As indicated by their definitions, there is a hierarchical relation between the four concepts. Individual work elements combine to delineate specific tasks, while a collection of related tasks constitutes a competency. And finally, a collection of tasks and competencies constitutes a work position. This relation between the four job analysis concepts is delineated in Figure 5.

In the analysis of jobs it is necessary to determine what jobs are and their precise limits; that is, where the jobs begin and where they end. The analyst must be able to analyze a group of positions, determine the number of jobs existing among the positions, and then determine the exact nature of these jobs.

Jobs should be analyzed as they exist; therefore, each completed job analysis study must report the job as it exists at the time of the analysis, not as it should exist, not as it has existed in the past, and not as it exists in similar local educational agencies.

Generally, in describing the tasks that comprise a job, the analyst should arrange them in either a chronological or a functional order. Tasks are usually arranged functionally when a job has no regular cycle of operations.

Basically, every job analysis should represent a description of one job. Tasks temporarily assigned to a given worker in addition to his regular duties should not be considered part of the basic job. The following are the kinds of situations which the analyst encounters in job analysis studies:

- The worker performs a specific cycle or sequence of operations. The analyst should begin with first task the worker is called upon to do and consider the work steps successively. For example, tasks for the preparation of audio-visual materials may be arranged in the following order: (a) sets up 16mm motion picture projector, (b) operates 16mm motion picture projector, (c) maintains 16mm motion picture projector films, (d) maintains supplemental equipment such as film screen, and (e) maintains and stores 16mm motion picture projector.
- The worker has no regular cycle of operations. This situation is usually more difficult to analyze since it frequently involves a considerable variety of tasks. The analyst should organize the information according to function. For example, a teacher of the secondary level mentally retarded should: (a) be able to select and utilize appropriate media to assist in classroom communication, (b) be able to design and produce selected audio-visual materials, (c) be able to identify, through the application of learning theory, the role of audio-visual materials in classroom communication, and (d) demonstrate an ability to operate selected audio-visual equipment. The above functions could be grouped under the headings of: (a) comparing and operating, (b) analyzing, synthesizing, and operating, (c) synthesizing, and (d) operating-controlling. The analyst should also study the work activities involved in the performance of these functions. If comparing and operating involves sorting, inspecting, selecting, examining, verifying, modifying, and regulating audio-visual materials for classroom use, the analyst should obtain sufficient data to explain the methods of accomplishing these activities.

Figure 5

Delineation of Job Analysis Concepts

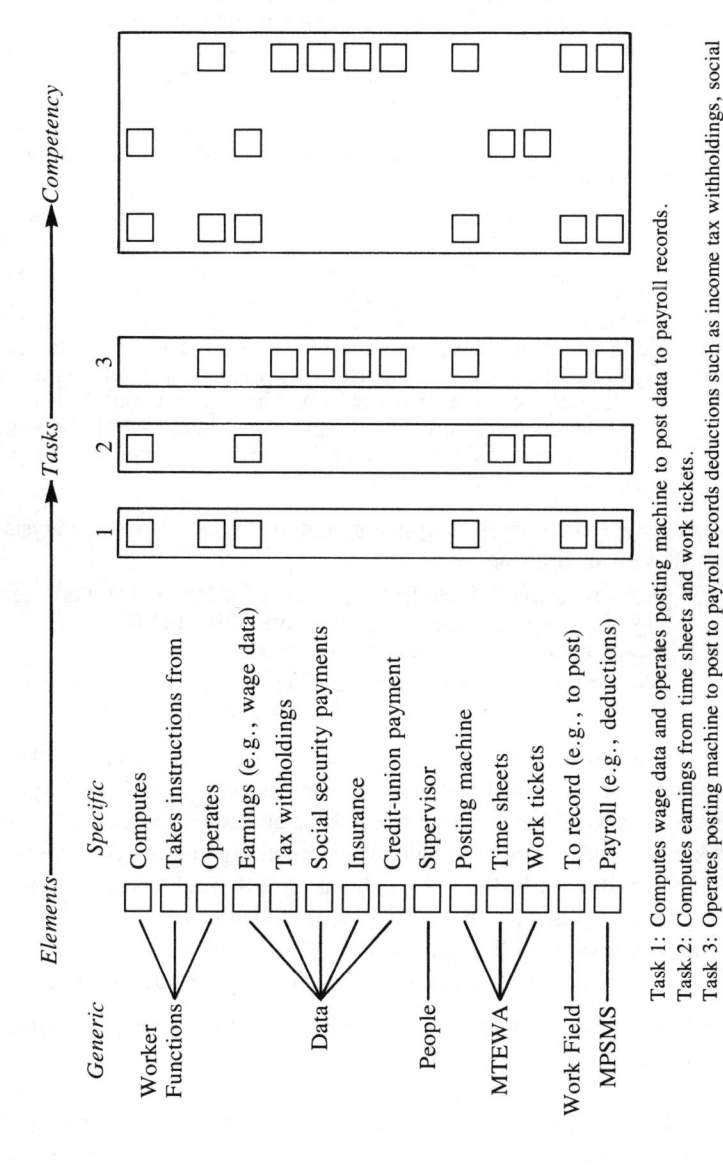

Elements ──────▶ *Tasks* ──────▶ *Competency*

Generic	Specific
Worker Functions	Computes
	Takes instructions from
	Operates
Data	Earnings (e.g., wage data)
	Tax withholdings
	Social security payments
	Insurance
	Credit-union payment
People	Supervisor
MTEWA	Posting machine
	Time sheets
	Work tickets
Work Field	To record (e.g., to post)
MPSMS	Payroll (e.g., deductions)

Task 1: Computes wage data and operates posting machine to post data to payroll records.
Task 2: Computes earnings from time sheets and work tickets.
Task 3: Operates posting machine to post to payroll records deductions such as income tax withholdings, social security payments, insurances, credit-union payments.
Competency: Public school central office accountant computes data and operates machinery and equipment for recording personnel financial information.

- The worker frequently changes from one set of tasks to another. For example, four teachers of the secondary level educable mentally retarded are found performing a set of duties which include: (a) instructing students in family living roles, functions and structures, (b) supervising physical education for handicapped students, (c) operating industrial craft tools, equipment and materials, and (d) comparing different methods of storing clothing using techniques and information available to retarded youth. The four teachers frequently alternate activities in accordance with specific instructional schedules. The tasks should ordinarily be analyzed collectively and recorded on one job analysis schedule, since the tasks involved, although performed by individual workers, actually constitute one job, all phases of which are performed by all the workers.
- The worker performs a given set of tasks although in emergencies he performes other sets of tasks involved in other jobs. For example, teachers of elementary level educable mentally retarded students and teachers of secondary level educable mentally retarded students provide instruction to handicapped students. Although the jobs are interchangable to the extent that any one of the teachers can perform the duties of any one of the teachers can perform the duties of any one of the others in emergencies, each teacher performs his respective job based on regularly scheduled activities. Situations such as these should be considered separate jobs, and the analyses should be recorded on separate job analysis schedules.

Five categories of job analysis elements are required for the analysis of any job. These categories are:
- Work performed, including (a) worker functions, (b) work fields, (c) machines, tools, equipment, and work aids, and (d) materials, products, subject matter, and services; and
- Worker traits, including training time, aptitudes, temperaments, interests, and physical demands and environmental conditions.

All job-worker situations (e.g., functioning of the worker in relationship to a specific set of tasks) involve to some degree a relationship on the part of the worker to data, people, and things. These relationships can be expressed by 24 worker functions arranged in hierarchies according to level; the lower the rank ordering, the higher the level. A combination of the highest functions which the worker performs in relation to data, people, and things expresses the total level of complexity for the job-worker situation. Schematically presented in Figure 6 is the structure of worker functions utilized by the U.S. Department of Labor.

Work fields are organizations of specific methods either (a) characteristic of machines, tools, equipment, or work aids, and directed at common technological objectives, or (b) characteristic of the techniques designed to fulfill socio-economic purposes. One hundred work fields have been organized by the U.S. Department of Labor for the purpose of classifying all forms of jobs. Each work field has a title, definition, and code number.

Work fields range from the specific (drafting, riveting, and sawing) to the general (structural-fabricating-installing-repairing). Usually general work fields are defined in terms of the less complex work fields that are specific to

Figure 6

Structure of Worker Functions

Data	People	Things
0 Synthesizing	0 Mentoring	0 Setting up
1 Coordinating	1 Negotiating	1 Precision working
2 Analyzing	2 Instructing	2 Operating-controlling
3 Compiling	3 Supervising	3 Driving-operating
4 Computing	4 Diverting	4 Manipulating
5 Copying	5 Persuading	5 Tending
6 Comparing	6 Speaking-signaling	6 Feeding-offbearing
	7 Serving	7 Handling
	8 Taking instructions-helping	

them. For example, educational administration can be defined as a work field which includes combinations of the specific work field methods of analyzing, contracting, directing, interviewing, negotiating, planning, scheduling, and supervising.

Although a job may involve techniques specific to a number of work fields it should be characterized in terms of primary involvement. For example, the job of educational administration, which includes supervisory duties, may also include scheduling duties relative to those supervisory duties. However, in the case of the educational administrative job of special education supervisor of mentally retarded students, the primary work field involvement would be supervision, with the work field of scheduling subsidiary.

Work fields are organized into groups on the basis of similar overall objectives, such as processing of materials, fabrication of products, utilization of data, and the provision of services. Each work field should be followed by a list of methods verbs and its characteristic machines, tools, equipment, and work aids. Methods verbs are verbs which are used to denote the specific methods of performing the work. They are indicative of how the objectives of the work field are accomplished and relate to the technologies and knowledge areas basic to the specific work fields. Some of these verbs occur in more than one work field and their meanings may change accordingly. The machines, tools, equipment, and work aids are those instruments and devices which are used to carry out the specific functions. These instruments and devices are defined as follows:

- Machines: devices which are a combination of mechanical parts with the framework and fastenings to support and connect them, designed to apply a force to do work on or move materials or to process data. Relative to the work field of teaching, this category would include typewriters, adding machines or braille writers;

- Tools: implements which are manipulated to do work on or move materials. Included are all common hand tools, plus those manipulated by the worker and motivated by outside power sources, such as electricity. For teaching, this category would include pens, pencils, pointers, slate and stylus.

- Equipment: devices which generate power, communicate signals, or have an effect upon material through the application of light, heat, electricity, steam, chemicals, or atmospheric pressure. For teaching, this category would include projectors, public address systems, and tape recorders. Also included in this category are non-processing devices, such as prosthetic devices and wheel chairs; and

- Work aids: miscellaneous items which cannot be considered as machines, tools, or equipment, and yet are necessary for carrying out the work. For teaching, this category would include blackboards, chalk, charts, diagrams, examinations, manuals, maps, publications, reference books, and textbooks.

Materials, products, subject matter, and services include: (a) basic materials being processed, such as fabric, metal, or wood, (b) final products being made such as dresses or wood craft objects, (c) data, when being dealt with or applied such English or geometry, and (d) services, such as bus driving or janitorial services. In organization and content, materials, products, subject matter, and services can be categorized in accordance with the *Standard Industrial Classification Manual*[51] and the *Standard Terminology for Curriculum and Instruction in Local and State School Systems.*[52] Categories of tangibles are those which cover materials and products (e.g., wood craft products). Categories of intangibles are those involving specialized knowledge which cannot be expressed in terms of a material or products (e.g., business services and administration).

The technique devised to assist the analyst in stating a job-worker situation has been developed into a standard, concise form. By applying the technique of sentence analysis to job analysis, a model for expressing a job-worker situation emerges appropriate for us by local educational agencies. This technique permits the most complex job-worker situation to be stated in brief declarative sentences.

In order to follow the steps in this technique, notice that the framework for the sentence analysis is constant: (a) an implied subject, (b) verb (c) object, and (d) modifying infinitive phrase. More specifically,

- The subject is always the worker (implied but not expressed);
- The verb, which always begins the sentence, is synonymous with the worker function;
- The immediate object is either data, people, or materials, tools, equipment, and work aids. Also, in case of: (a) data function, the object is information in some form, (b) people function, the object is usually the people to whom a service is being rendered, and (c) thing function, the object is a machine, tool, equipment or work aid through which the action of the verb is performed; and
- The infinitive phrase has a varying influence as a modifier so that the

infinitive is the work field, and the object of the infinitive is materials, products, subject matter, and services.

Following is a job-worker situation applicable to teachers of secondary level educable mentally retarded students.

Designs instructional materials to fit specific teaching objectives. This includes: (a) creating non-projected, projected, three-dimensional, and reading materials, (b) producing nonphotographic transparencies, (c) preparing audio materials, and (d) developing and cataloging a community resource and vertical resource file.

The requirements made on the worker in terms of aptitudes, general educational development, vocational preparation, physical demands, and personal traits are expressed by worker traits. These are reflected in the following components:

- Training time;
- Aptitudes;
- Temperaments;
- Interests; and
- Physical demands and environmental conditions.

Data relating to these job facets provide a sharper focus on the type of work involved and the nature of the individual worker. They are extremely beneficial in counseling, job development and redesign, training, and other activities directed toward maximum manpower utilization, especially for less-than-fully qualified persons. The following are the definitions utilized by the U.S. Department of Labor for worker traits components:

- Training time: The amount of general educational development and specific vocational preparation required of a worker to acquire the knowledge and abilities necessary for average performance in a particular job-worker situation. Training time includes: (a) general educational development, which involves those aspects of education, both formal and informal, that contribute to the worker's reasoning development and ability to follow instruction, and acquisition of "tool" knowledge, such as language and mathematical skills, and (b) specific vocational preparation: the amount of time required to learn the techniques, acquire information, and develop the facility needed for average performance in a specific jobworker situation. The training may be acquired in a school, work, military, institutional, or avocational environment;

- Aptitudes: the specific capacities or abilities required of an individual in order to facilitate the learning of some task or job duty. Following are the aptitudes included in this component: (a) intelligence, (b) verbal, (c) numerical, (d) spatial, (e) form perception, (f) clerical perception, (g) motor coordination, (h) finger dexterity, (i) manual dexterity, (j) eye-hand-foot coordination, and (k) color discrimination;

- Temperaments: the "personal traits" required of a worker by specific job-worker situations. This component consists of the following factors: (a) adaptability to accepting responsibility for the direction, control, or planning of an activity, (b) adaptability to situations involving the interpretation of feelings, ideas, or facts in terms of personal viewpoint, (c) adaptability to influencing people in their opinions, attitudes, or judgments about ideas or things, (d) adaptability to making generalizations, evaluations, or decisions based on sensory judgmental criteria, (e) adaptability to making generalizations, evaluations, or decisions based on measurable or verifiable criteria, (f) adaptability to dealing with people beyond giving and receiving instructions, (g) adaptability to performing repetitive work, or to performing continuously the same work, according to set procedures, sequence, or pace (h) adaptability to performing under stress when confronted with emergency critical, unusual, or dangerous situations; or situations in which working speed and sustained attention are make-or-break aspects of the job, (i) adaptability to situations requiring the precise attainment of set limits, tolerances, or standards, and (j) adaptability to performing a variety of duties, often changing from one task to another of a different nature without loss of efficiency or composure.

Bingham defined interests are "a tendency to become absorbed in an experience and to continue it, while an aversion is a tendency to turn away from it to something else."[53] The U.S. Department of Labor utilized five basic interest factors dichotomized as follows:

- A preference for activities dealing with things and objects;
- A preference for activities involving business contact with people;
- A preference for activities of a routine, concrete, organized nature;
- A preference for working for the presumed good of people;
- A preference for activities resulting in prestige or the esteem of others.

- A preference for activities concerned with the communication of data;
- A preference for activities of a scientific and technical nature;
- A preference for activities of an abstract and creative nature;
- A preference for activities that are carried on in relation to processes, machines, and techniques;
- A preference for activities resulting in tangible, productive satisfaction.

Physical demands are defined as the physical requirements made of the worker by the specific job-worker situation. They include:
- Strength (i.e., lifting, carrying, pushing, and/or pulling) relative to the continuum of sedentary, light, medium, heavy, and very heavy work;
- Climbing and/or balancing;
- Reaching, handling, fingering, and/or feeling;
- Talking and/or hearing;
- Seeing.

Environmental conditions are those physical surroundings of job-worker situations which make specific demands upon a worker's physical capacity. They include: (a) work location (e.g., inside, outside, or both), (b) extreme cold with or without temperature changes, (c) extreme heat with or without temperature changes, (d) wet and/or humid atmospheric conditions, (e) noise and/or vibration, (f) hazards, and (g) other atmospheric conditions.

In summary, there are five categories of job analysis elements required for the analysis of any job: (a) worker functions, (b) work fields, (c) machines, tools, equipment, and work aids, (d) materials, products, subject matter, and services, and (e) worker traits. By employing these five categories of job analysis elements, the self-evaluation coordinator and the local educational agency will be able to delineate the salient worker-job environmental components. Furthermore, this information can be used to redesign job specifications to accommodate qualified handicapped workers.

Conceptual delineation of job analysis components. This portion of Chapter II describes planning, conducting, and analyzing procedures that can be followed by the self-evaluation coordinator in conducting a job analysis study (Phase IVa: Implementation of the self-evaluation design). The techniques used will secure detailed, valid, and authoritative job information. The basic job analysis approach described is a combination of three data gathering techniques: (a) observation, (b) questioning/interviewing, and (c) measurement techniques. Delineated in Figure 7 are the specific planning, conducting, and analyzing components of a job analysis.

The planning component of the job analysis involves nine basic decision steps. These include:
- Determining the job analysis to be conducted;
- Determining who will conduct the job analysis;
- Determining the job analysis populations and sampling procedures;
- Determining managerial/worker logistical issues and problems;
- Determining the job analysis methodological approaches;
- Determining the job analysis variables;
- Determining the current job status based on job description;
- Develop the job analysis instrument; and
- Determine the data analysis methods.

In determining the job analysis to be conducted, there are two fundamental questions that need to be addressed by the self-evaluation coordinator:
- Is the job analysis concerned with a specific job within a specific educational setting (e.g., the assistant principals position at Dunbar Elementary School), or concerned with a generic job category applicable to a variety of educational settings (e.g., eight elementary school teachers to meet manpower vacancy projections for the next school year)?
- To whom are the results of the job analysis to be delivered (e.g., the principal of Dunbar Elementary School or the Director of Personnel who will be responsible for employing elementary school teachers)?

In determining who will conduct the job analysis, there are five fundamental questions that need to be addressed by the self-evaluation coordinator:

Figure 7

The Planning, Conducting, and Analyzing Components of a Job Analysis

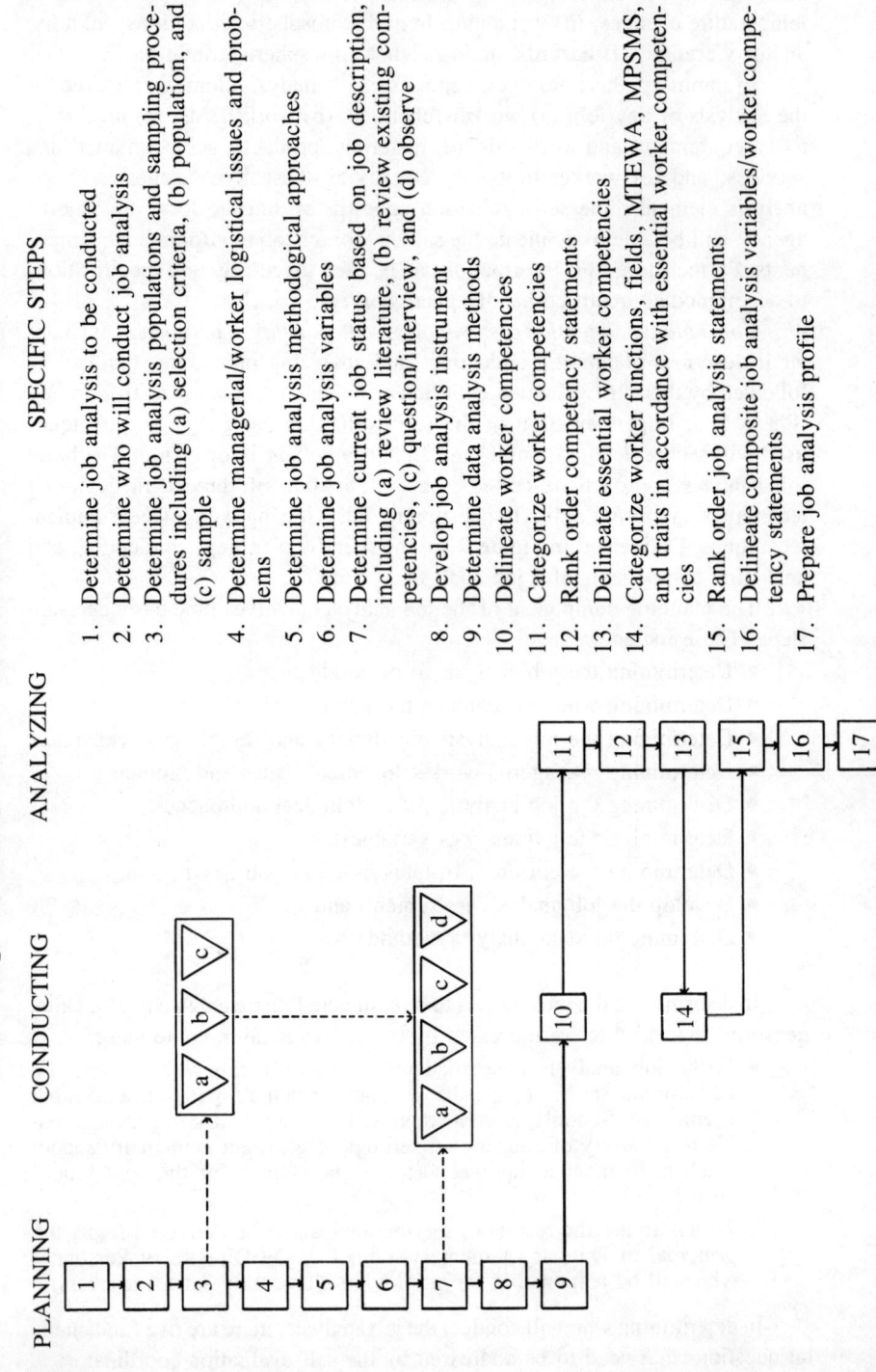

PLANNING CONDUCTING ANALYZING SPECIFIC STEPS

1. Determine job analysis to be conducted
2. Determine who will conduct job analysis
3. Determine job analysis populations and sampling procedures including (a) selection criteria, (b) population, and (c) sample
4. Determine managerial/worker logistical issues and problems
5. Determine job analysis methodological approaches
6. Determine job analysis variables
7. Determine current job status based on job description, including (a) review literature, (b) review existing competencies, (c) question/interview, and (d) observe
8. Develop job analysis instrument
9. Determine data analysis methods
10. Delineate worker competencies
11. Categorize worker competencies
12. Rank order competency statements
13. Delineate essential worker competencies
14. Categorize worker functions, fields, MTEWA, MPSMS, and traits in accordance with essential worker competencies
15. Rank order job analysis statements
16. Delineate composite job analysis variables/worker competency statements
17. Prepare job analysis profile

- Should the job analysis be conducted by personnel employed by the local educational agency or should services be contracted through an institution of higher learning, state department of education, intermediate administrative unit, or regional educational agency?
- Is it appropriate and feasible for the self-evaluation coordinator to conduct the job analysis study?
- What are the professional competencies necessary to conduct a job analysis?
- Are there social, political, or economical restrictions that will limit the range of individuals who can conduct the job analysis?
- Who has the legal authority to negotiate for the services of a job analyst?

In determining the job populations to be analyzed and the sampling procedures to be used, there are thirteen fundamental questions that need to be addressed by the self-evaluation coordinator:

- How does the selection of the job analysis to be conducted delimit the populations and samples to be used?
- Who are those individuals who comprise the universe of all relevant employees to be studied or utilized in the study?
- How are the populations and samples selected and what are the identifiable characteristics of each population?
- Who are those individuals that constitute the invited sample (that group from the total population to which an invitation to participate is extended)?
- Who are those individuals that constitute the accepting sample (that portion of the invited sample that accepts the invitation and agrees to participate)?
- Who are those individuals that constitute the data-producing sample (that portion of the accepting sample that actually produces data)?
- Will the sampling process use constant or proportional selection?
- If the job analysis study concerns a generic job category applicable to a variety of educational settings, (a) How representative are the selected populations and samples? and (b) What selection procedures are to be used (i.e., random, systematic, deliberate, or cluster)?
- If the job analysis study concerns a specific job within a specific educational setting, who are those individuals or groups, other than the individual currently engaged in that position, that should participate in the job analysis?
- If the job analysis concerns a generic job category applicable to a variety of educational settings, who are those persons or groups, other than the group being studied, that should participate in the job analysis?
- How should these individuals or groups participate, and who determines whether or not these individuals or groups do participate?
- What "weight" is to be given to those other individuals or groups descriptions, judgments, and opinions concerning a specific job situation or generic job category?
- What financial and logistical problems are involved in the sampling process decided upon?

In determining the managerial/worker logistical issues and problems in conducting the job analysis, there are six fundamental questions that need to be addressed by the self-evaluation coordinator:
- How much will the job analysis study cost?
- What local or state funds are available for use by the school system and the analyst?
- How cooperative will the individuals and groups involved in the study be in terms of completing the study?
- What are the political and social restraints placed on the analyst?
- What are the resource requirements necessary for conducting the job analysis study?
- Are there local or state policies, regulations, or laws that can restrict the activities of the job analyst?

Although there are a variety of data gathering techniques that can be employed for describing work environments, the author recommends the two descriptive techniques of (a) observation and (b) questioning/interviewing. In a discussion of the techniques for the analysis of qualitative data, Fox notes that "when the [job analyst] has collected verbal or behavioral data through observational, measuring, or questioning techniques like . . . critical incident questions, he is faced with a difficult problem of data analysis."[54] Verbal responses to questions or interviews and descriptions concerning employee behavior not only do not lend themselves to immediate analysis, but also do not provide sufficient information so as to comply with Federal guidelines for employment selection. Furthermore, most school districts lack the technical capability and financial resources necessary to conduct a highly sophisticated statistical analysis of specific work behaviors. Any job analysis approach should: (a) have a high probability of success, (b) be economical in terms of direct and indirect financial expenditures, (c) provide detailed and accurate information for personnel decision-making and manpower planning, (d) be flexible enough to be used with a variety of organizational situations, and (e) employ statistical tests and research designs that school personnel can understand and use without extensive training. A combination of the two descriptive techniques meets these criteria.

The questioning method has several advantages:
- It is a direct method of obtaining information from a worker;
- Direct questioning is particularly appropriate at the surface and subsurface levels of job analysis;
- The questioning method can be effectively used with a variety of survey approaches;
- Depending on which questioning technique used (e.g., check list or structured questionnaire), a substantial amount of data can be accumulated rapidly and conveniently; and
- It is economical in terms of direct and indirect financial expenditures.

Listed below is the sequence of steps, developed from recommendations by Fox,[55] to be followed in applying the method of questioning to a job analysis study.

- Determination that the questioning method is appropriate;
- Identification of the areas of content for questioning;
- Identification of the full range of specific questions which might be used;
- Initial classification of potential questions into those considered critical for the job analysis and those not critical;
- Identification of demands of the job analysis in terms of analyst-respondent interaction;
- Identification of the limits in respondent contacts;
- Determination of the kinds of questions to be used and the format of the answers;
- Selection of the technique for questioning;
- Development of the instrument for questioning;
- Pilot studies to determine the characteristics of the instrument;
- Implementation of the data-gathering plan; and
- Include data results in job analysis report.

The conceptual delineation of techniques for questioning as a function of the analyst-worker interaction and the response format is presented in Figure 8.

Figure 8[56]
Concept Delineation of Techniques for Questioning as a Function of the Analyst-Worker Interaction and the Response Format

Type Of Response Format	Nature of Analyst-Worker Interaction		
	Impersonal or Mixed		Personal
Totally Structured	Check List	Structured Questionnaire	Structured Interview
Structured, With Free Option		Structured Questionnaire	Structured Interview
Limited Free	Critical Incident	Unstructured Questionnaire	Unstructured Interview
Totally Free		Unstructured Questionnaire	Unstructured Interview

Generic Job Category ↓ Specific Job

As delineated in Figure 8, an analysis of a generic job category applicable to a variety of educational settings will usually require the use of more structured response formats and impersonal analyst-worker interaction, and conversely, an analysis of a specific job within a specific educational setting will usually require the use of more non-structured response formats and personal analyst-worker interaction. Regardless of the questioning approach used, however, the purpose of questioning school personnel is to obtain all the information necessary for the job analysis.

If the questioning technique to be used is an interview, the following "rules-of-thumb" should be considered:

- Put the worker at ease by learning his/her name in advance, introducing yourself, and discussing general and pleasant topics long enough to establish rapport;
- Make the purpose of the interview clear by explaining why the interview was scheduled, what is expected to be accomplished, and how the workers cooperation will help in the production of occupational analysis tools used for placement and counseling of qualified handicapped workers. Assure the worker that the interview is not concerned with time study or wages;
- Encourage the worker to talk by always being courteous and showing a sincere interest in what he/she says;
- Help the worker to think and talk according to the logical sequence of the duties performed. If duties are not performed in a regular order, ask the worker to describe and list (by priority) the duties in a functional manner. Request the worker to describe the infrequent duties of his job, ones that are not part of his regular activities. Infrequently performed duties, however, should not include periodic or emergency activities such as an annual supplies inventory or providing emergency medical treatment to a student;
- Allow the worker sufficient time to answer each question and to formulate an answer. The analyst should discuss only one issue or ask one question at a time;
- Phrase questions carefully so that the answers will be more than "yes" or "no";
- Leading questions should be avoided;
- Secure specific and complete information pertaining to the two categories of information required for a complete analysis of a job (i.e., work performed and worker traits);
- Conduct the interview in plain, easily understood language;
- Consider the relationship of the job under analysis to other jobs in the school, program, project, or central office;
- Control the interview with respect to the economic use of time and adherence to subject matter;
- The interview should be conducted patiently and with consideration for any nervousness or lack of ease on the part of the worker;
- In closing the interview, summarize the information obtained from the worker indicating the major duties performed and the details concerning each of the duties; and
- Close the interview on a friendly note.

Several practical miscellaneous "does and don'ts" for interviews includes:
- Do not take issue with the worker's statements;
- Do not display any partiality to grievances or conflicts concerning the employer-employee relations;
- Do not display any interest in the wage classification of the job;
- Do not "talk down" to the worker;
- Do not permit the analyst to be influenced by personal likes and dislikes;
- Do not be critical or attempt to suggest any changes or improvements in organization or methods or work;
- Talk to the worker only with permission of his supervisor;
- Verify job data, especially instructional, curricular, and psychological information; and
- Verify completed analysis with proper school authorities.

The analyst must develop a certain skill in combining note taking with the conversational aspect of the interview. He must be able to write intelligible notes while engaged in conversation or to intersperse writing with fluent conversation. Often in deference to the analyst, the worker will stop talking while notes are being made. The analyst should clarify whether he wishes the conversation continued or not in these circumstances.

Some workers display hesitancy or openly object to a record (especially tape recordings) being made of what they say. The analyst must decide how much the interview may be effected by this attitude and modify his practices accordingly. If a tape recording is not possible or inappropriate, a small looseleaf book such as a stenographer's notebook is best suited for recording notes while interviewing. Suggestions for effective note taking include:
- Notes should be complete, legible and contain data necessary for the preparation of the job analysis schedule;
- Notes should be organized logically according to job tasks and the categories of information required for a complete analysis; and
- Notes should include only the facts about the job with emphasis on the work performed and worker traits involved. Use only words, phrases, and sentences that impart necessary information.

While the questioning method has several advantages, it has one important disadvantage. By posing a question for the respondent, the analyst must assume that the relation between a respondent's perception of a job analysis situation is highly correlated with actual worker behaviors and traits. When the number of respondents being questioned is large, this disadvantage can be minimal; however, when the number of respondents being questioned is limited, misperception of worker behaviors and traits can adversely affect a job analysis study.

With the observation method the analyst is basically concerned with a straightforward description of the job analysis situation. With the exception of observer bias, the observation method can avoid respondent misperceptions of worker behavior. As Fox notes, "when it is appropriate, the observation method will produce a kind of data which . . . other . . . methods cannot, for the raw material of observation is reality itself."

Listed below is the sequence of steps to be followed in applying the method of observation to a job analysis study.[57]

- Statement of the job analysis to be conducted and the information sufficient for delineation of the job situation;
- Determination that observation is appropriate and required;
- Specification of outcomes and content of the observation;
- Identification of the selected sample of job analysis situations;
- Consideration of characteristics of the job analysis situation in conjunction with the content to determine the elements of the observation (i.e., direct versus indirect observation; known versus unknown observation; role of the observer);
- Consideration of observation content and desired interaction to determine the choice of experienced versus inexperienced observers;
- Selection of observation technique;
- Recruitment of observers;
- Development of observation guide (based on experienced-inexperienced observers);
- Training of observers for sufficient reliability;
- Pilot studies to (a) provide observers with field experience in the use of the observation guide, (b) provide data to estimate reliability of the guide, (c) provide test of data analysis plan, and (d) verify that data will answer job analysis questions;
- Design of the observation data-gathering plan;
- Invitation to selected sample to participate;
- Implementation of data-gathering plan;
- Analysis of data; and
- Include data results in job analysis report.

In determining the job analysis variables to be included in the study, there are seven fundamental questions that need to be addressed by the self-evaluation coordinator:

- Who determines the job analysis variables to be included in the study?
- Are the Department of Labor's job analysis variables inclusive for all pertinent worker variables?
- Are there critical incidents that sufficiently and appropriately define each job analysis variable within the context of specific work environments?
- What methodological approaches are appropriate for describing work environment critical incidents?
- Can each of the pertinent worker variables be used to delineate specific worker tasks?
- Can each of the pertinent worker variables be used to delineate specific worker competencies?
- Can each of the pertinent worker variables be "translated" from existing employee competencies into specific job analysis sentences (i.e., tasks)?

In determining the current status of the job to be analyzed based on job descriptions, there are three fundamental questions that need to be addressed by the self-evaluation coordinator:
- How has the job to be analyzed been described by the school system (e.g., an outline of job responsibilities or a set of specific job competencies)?
- How concise and inclusive is the job description?
- How accurate are current job descriptions in comparison with actual job performance?

In developing the job analysis instruments, there are five fundamental questions that need to be addressed by the self-evaluation coordinator:
- How will the job analysis data gathering techniques to be used influence a job analysis instrument?
- What financial, personnel, or logistical problems are involved in developing the job analysis instrument?
- How reliable, valid, sensitive, appropriate, and objective is the job analysis instrument?
- What previous job analyses have been conducted and what techniques and instruments were employed?
- If there is no relevant previous use of the job analysis instrument, then has the analyst conducted sufficient pilot studies so that the combination of the pilot data and his and others experience forms a sensible foundation for the content of the instrument?

In addition to these five questions, the job analysis instrument should include:
- A directory of definitions for *all* pertinent job analysis variables. This can be obtained from the U.S. Department of Labor's *Handbook for Analyzing Jobs;* and[58]
- A list of specific worker competencies.

In determining the data analysis methods to be used in the study, there are four fundamental questions that need to be addressed by the self-evaluation coordinator:
- What descriptive or inferential statistical techniques need to be used for the job analysis study?
- Will the statistical tests and job design provide detailed and accurate information for personnel decision-making and manpower planning?
- Are the statistical tests and job analysis design such that school personnel can understand and use them without extensive training?
- Do the statistical tests and job analysis design meet EEOC guidelines?

The conducting and analyzing components of the job analysis involves eight decision steps. These include:
- Delineating worker competencies;
- Categorizing worker competencies;
- Rank ordering competency statements;

- Delineating essential worker competencies;
- Categorizing worker functions, fields, materials, tools, equipment, work aids, machines, products, subject matter, services and traits in accordance with essential worker competencies;
- Rank ordering job analysis statements;
- Delineating composite job analysis/worker competency statements; and
- Preparing the job analysis profile.

An examination of each of these eight conducting and analyzing components follows.

From reviewing the literature, reviewing existing competencies, questioning/interviewing, and observing a select number of school personnel engaged in job related activities, the job analyst is ready to delineate a list of specific worker competencies. If the list of worker competencies to be used is small (i.e., 30 or fewer items), then the job analyst can personally arrange the competencies into generic competency categories (e.g., five competencies related to instructional strategies, five competencies related to personalized curricula). However, if the list of worker competencies to be used is large (i.e., more than 30 items), the job analyst should request that the competency statements be reviewed by a select group of individuals with expertise in the applicable job area. This select group of experts should perform three activities: (a) critique the listing for clarity and check for omissions or redundances, (b) sort the statements into generic competency categories, and (c) judge how well each item represents the assigned category. Once a final listing of competencies is obtained, the job analyst should incorporate these competencies into the job analysis instrument.

Steps eleven through thirteen require sample participants to work with competency statements, while steps fourteen through sixteen require sample participants to work with composite job analysis variable/worker competency statements. Unless logistical problems dictate otherwise, steps eleven through thirteen should be conducted at one time, while steps fourteen through sixteen should be conducted at another time (preferably immediately following the first time).

After a final listing of competencies is obtained, the job analyst should administer the job analysis instrument to the selected worker sample. Day one procedures include: (a) distribute the list of competencies, (b) briefly review each competency, (c) answer any questions concerning any competency, (d) request that sample participants assign each competency statement to any of the generic competency categories (e.g., professional knowledge, classroom climate, etc.), (e) request that sample participants rate on a Likert scale (1-5) the degree of relevance the competency has to the assigned category (relevancy should be defined in terms of participant perceptions of individual "on-job" behavior), and (f) collecting the set of competencies. The job analyst then rank-orders the competency statements on the basis of the median ratings. The five highest ranked competencies in each category are used to define the category. At this point, the job analyst incorporates the remaining competencies into the job analysis instrument. The job analysis instrument now contains the essential worker competencies matriced with job analysis variables.

Day two procedures include: (a) distribute the directory of definitions for job analysis variables, (b) review each definition, (c) answer any questions concerning any term or definition, (d) review the results of the competency list ranking, (e) distribute the job analysis instrument, (f) request that sample participants rate on a Likert scale (1-5) the degree of relevancy the competency has to each specific job analysis variable (relevancy should be defined in terms of participant perceptions of the value of each specific job analysis variable relative to each competency), and (g) collecting the job analysis instrument. The job analyst then rank orders each specific job analysis variable/competency on the basis of the median ratings. Those specific job analysis variables with a group median score of between 3.0 and 5.0 are used to define the generic job analysis element categories.

The final step in the job analysis study is the preparation of the job analysis profile. The job analysis profile should include: (a) basic descriptive data, including the job that was analyzed, date of analysis, job analyst's name, address, and telephone number, job analysis population, sample and sample size, (b) list of competencies by category (rank ordered), and (c) compilation sheet delineating median scores for specific job analysis variables/worker competencies.

Organizational structure and operation analysis. The narrative report is to a local educational agency what an introductory statement is to a definition. A good narrative report provides the context in which the particular job analysis study was made and serves to orient decision-makers to the circumstance under which a specific job exists at a specific time within the context of a specific organization. This supplemental information is especially important to the personnel decision-makers before he examines the individual job analysis profile. Further, the narrative report provides broad general occupational information which cannot be properly included in the job analysis profile.

The information in a narrative report grows out of discussions with school personnel (e.g., teachers, psychologists, guidance counselors, etc.), administrators (e.g., principals, directors, supervisors, coordinators, etc.), educational experts, industry experts, university and college personnel. Also, literature pertaining to the local educational agency is reviewed. The job analyst makes inquiries concerning the structure and operation of the local educational agency, the job interrelationships (i.e., type of formal/informal organizational attributes; authority characteristics; planning/programming, control and information systems), motivation and incentive characteristics, organizational style and climate, leadership characteristics, decision-making style, communication networks, staffing procedures and any other issues or topics which he feels will contribute to understanding the worker-job interaction and environment. Much of this information can be obtained during the job analysis phase of activities.

Examples of the kind of questions for which the job analyst should seek answers are:

- What is the purpose of the job?
- What is the nature of the service rendered?
- What knowledge or technologies are required for adequate performance?
- How is the service rendered?
- What are the general duties or procedures?
- What are the general environmental conditions?
- What are the hazards encountered by school personnel?
- What working conditions are peculiar to the job being analyzed?
- Are the services or work flow of the local educational agency divided into departments or units, and if so, how?
- How are these units interrelated, or how are they arranged in a work flow process?
- What are the personnel staffing practices?
- Are women, racial/ethnic minorities, and handicapped school personnel used in a variety of positions and jobs, including the job being analyzed? What is the trend in regard to such workers? Does a form of career lattice exist in the district?
- Are inservice training activities provided by the local educational agency?
- Does this local educational agency have any unique characteristics in comparison to other districts in the area?
- What is the history of the development of the local educational agency?
- Has it initiated any progressive or unusual service delivery processes, equipment, projects, or services?
- What effects have these new ideas or projects had on the activities and employment status of school personnel in general, and handicapped personnel in particular?

Generally, the data obtained through the discussions with local educational agency personnel or other educational experts will fall fairly obviously under several major headings. Liberal use of such headings and their subheadings, even in a very short report, provides the decision-maker with a ready reference to the particular sections of the report and an easier to read, more interesting text. In addition, the use of headings helps the analyst to organize his materials in terms of the headings and helps him set limits on the amount of information included in the narrative.

A standard formula for organizing the report is neither possible nor desirable, as each report and each analyst's presentation will include many different types of data. However, a few general headings have been found to be significant in most reports. The following outline presents these headings, or it may include additional headings. The general headings are:

- Introduction or purpose of the local education agency, including (a) purpose, (b) scope and/or limit of study, and (c) history and/or development of the pertinent programs of the local educational agency;

- Environmental conditions, including (a) description of physical facilities, (b) description of pertinent equipment, and (c) general environmental conditions and general working conditions;
- Organization and operations, including (a) departmentalization of the local educational agency and pertinent programs, (b) work flow activities, (c) processes (if non-educational), and (d) services (if educational);
- Personnel policies and practices, including (a) hiring practices and requirements, (b) recruitment and/or sources of school personnel, (c) methods of training with emphasis on in-service, (d) hiring of minorities, handicapped, and disadvantaged, (e) entry job salary and placements, (f) career lattices and/or promotional opportunities, (g) job restructuring, and (h) effects of accommodation on personnel;
- Other sections;
- Appendix and glossary.

The introduction or purpose of the local educational agency section should begin with a statement of the educational goals, objectives, and services of the district in general, and relevant programs in particular. If the job analysis study concerns physical plant/maintenance activities, this section would include a general discussion of the raw materials involved, the processes used, and the range and variety of products, equipment, machines, tools, and work aids used. If the job analysis study concerns educational service activities (e.g., teaching, support staff, administration), the section would include a description of the nature of the service, and to whom and how the service is rendered. This section may also include a history of the pertinent program or job; how it developed, and possibly some future plans of the program or job, or future trends in job status. And finally, any restrictions which the local district imposes on the study (such as logistical restraints) and which affect the preparation of the job analysis study, should be noted here.

The environmental conditions section should include a description of the layout of typical physical facilities (e.g., classrooms), complete with architectural dimensions, to give the decision-makers a picture of the physical arrangement of pertinent buildings, facilities, equipment, storage or related areas as they affect work flow. The narration in this section should also include information on equipment, machines, and/or tools used, and general working conditions. The description given here should be concerned with the overall job picture and should furnish information not contained in the individual job analysis profile.

An explanation of the program of the local educational agency gives the necessary orientation for reading the individual job analysis. This section should begin with a discussion of the units, processes or major activities, and with their interrelation or position in the work flow. This would then be followed by a breakdown of the units, processes, or activities into separate subheadings with more detailed descriptions of each. When this section is read in conjunction with the environmental conditions section, it should enable the reader to visualize the total work situation into which the worker fits.

Phase Va: Modifying current procedures and practices

Phase Va concerns modifying current local educational agency employment practices and procedures. At the conclusion of the job analysis study, the self-evaluation coordinator will have collected information concerning: (a) either a specific job within a specific educational setting, or a generic job category applicable to a variety of educational settings, and (b) the structure and operation of the local education agency. At this point, the self-evaluation coordinator can make specific recommendations concerning: (a) job-related accommodations needed to provide qualified handicapped individuals with appropriate employment opportunities, and (b) the degree of compliance between the local educational agencies personnel staffing process and Section 504, Subpart B regulation. Also at this point, the role and responsibilities of the self-evaluation coordinator can be either: (a) terminated while administrative decision-makers debate and/or implement the self-evaluator's recommendations and suggestions, or (b) altered in accordance with Scriven's goal-free evaluation approach so that the self-evaluation coordinator begins assisting in the developmental planning and implementing of alternate staffing practices and procedures.

Because the issues related to modifying a local education agencies employment practices and procedures are important for complying with Section 504 regulation, it is appropriate to address the problems of costs, benefits, and economic impact of implementing needed modifications. For this reason, the author has included O'Neill's (paraphrased and slightly modified) report *Discrimination Against Handicapped Persons: The Costs, Benefits and Economic Impact of Implementing Section 504 of the Rehabilitation Act of 1973 Concerning Recipients of HEW Financial Assistance.*[59] This report was originally published with proposed Section 504 regulation in the Federal Register on May 17, 1976.

> Although all the provisions of Subpart B are aimed at the same objective—assuring nondiscriminatory treatment of handicapped workers—Subpart B can be divided into two basic components. One component (Paragraphs 84.13 and 84.14) relates to the employer's recruitment, selection and promotion procedures and practices, while the other component (Paragraph 84.12) relates to the structure of the work situation, and requires that employer's make ". . . reasonable accommodation to the known physical or mental limitations of a handicapped applicant or employee unless the recipient can demonstrate that the accommodation would impose an undue hardship on the operation of the recipient's program." Reasonable accommodation includes: (a) adjustments such as making facilities readily accessible, (b) job restructuring, (c) parttime and modified work schedules, (d) acquisition or modification of equipment and devices, and (e) other similar actions. The determination of whether an accommodation will be required (e.g., whether undue hardship exists) will be based on such factors as the size and type of the recipient's operation and the nature and cost of the needed accommodations.

The provisions dealing with recruitment, selection and promotion procedures are designed to eliminate discriminatory practices without imposing any added cost (with the possible exception of minor administrative costs) upon recipients. For example, local educational agencies make routine preemployment inquires about the mental and physical condition of the applicant. The regulation would prohibit this practice but allow inquiry as to the applicant's ability to perform job-related functions.

This approach will especially aid those with the less visible handicapping conditions (e.g., epilepsy, diabetes, emotional problems). Many of these individuals are seriously inhibited in their job search because of the fear that they will be summarily rejected if they reveal their handicapping condition. For example, a teacher with epilepsy who could qualify for a principal's position may not apply because a minor accommodation may be required and he/she is afraid to reveal his/her condition. In this situation the individual's earnings capacity is reduced even though the local educational agency might have been willing to make the required accommodation. Thus, the procedural provisions by themselves, even without additional reasonable accommodations, will produce benefits in the form of increased earnings for handicapped workers. Since the cost imposed on employers by these procedural requirements will be negligible, Paragraph 84.13 and 84.14 regulation, when implemented, will be highly cost effective.

The reasonable accommodation provision (Paragraph 84.12) seeks to provide benefits to handicapped individuals by breaking down employment barriers due to ignorance and stereotyped thinking. It differs from the procedural provisions, however, in that it will require employers in some situations to incur additional costs at the outset in order for the handicapped workers to be equally productive. The phrases "in some situations" and "at the outset" are underlined to stress that for most combinations of types of handicapped condition and job category "reasonable accommodation" will require either no or only minor outlays. For example, it might involve no more than abandoning a misconception such as thinking that hiring a person with epilepsy will raise insurance rates. And in situations where outlays are required it will usually involve only minor initial investment rather than a major on-going outlay. For example, this might mean recognizing that the traditional job specifications are either outmoded or can be easily adapted to the particular type of handicap in question.

Of course, there are some situations where the types of accommodations that would be required can become a source of controversy. These situations are of two kinds. One involves disease entities that may or may not be in a stabilized condition. Diabetes and cancer are the two important types that occur in practice. Dispute can arise over what the actual probabilities of re-occurrence are and we will review that experience under Section 503 in connection with this issue.

The other class of situations involves the various kinds of emotional handicaps—psychotic reaction, depression, anxiety reaction, etc. The emotional handicaps differ sharply from the physical in how much they can be overcome by simple job restructuring and other kinds of minor accommodations. As shown in Figure 9, the effect of emotional handicaps on earnings is much greater than for many severe types of physical disabilities. It is not clear whether discrimination by employers is as major a factor in lowering earnings for the emotionally disturbed group as for the

Figure 9

Incidence of Work Disability by Severity of Disability, Sex and Age for Persons 18-64 Years Old: United States: 1970

Age	(1) Partially Work Disabled (000)	(2) Totally Work Disabled (000)	(3) Incidence: Percent of Population Work Disabled %	(4) Percent of Population Reporting Totally Work Disabled %	(5) Estimated* Percent Totally Work Disabled %	(6) Percent of Population Who Reported They Never Worked
Total (Both Sexes)						
All ages	7,160	4,931	10.8%	4.4%	4.0%	.9%
18-24	1,004	329	5.7	1.4	2.5	.7
25-54	4,135	2,358	9.3	3.3	11.5	2.1
55+	1,972	2,242	22.8	12.1		
Male						
All ages	4,356	2,010	11.7%	3.7%	3.2%	.5%
18-24	689	157	7.5	1.4	1.9	.4
25-54	2,470	911	9.9	2.7	9.9	.7
55+	1,178	941	24.2	10.7		
Female						
All ages	2,803	2,921	9.9%	5.0%	4.7%	1.3%
18-24	315	172	4.1	1.4	3.1	.9
25-54	1,694	1,448	8.6	4.0	12.9	3.4
55+	793	1,302	21.5	13.4		

*Only counts those who both reported themselves totally worked disabled *and* said they were not at work or seeking work.

Source: U.S. Bureau of the Census, Census of Population: 1975, *Subject Reports*, Final Report PC (2)-6C. Persons with Work Disability, U.S. Govt. Printing Office, Tables 1 and 4.

other group. In any case, the applicability of most of the known types of "reasonable accommodation" would appear to be limited for those with emotional handicaps.

The reasonable accommodation provision is likely to generate concern about possible significant cost increases. Therefore, the rest of this section is primarily devoted to presenting data and survey results on the probable costs of reasonable accommodation. First, however, evidence on pecuniary benefits (attributable to the entire subpart) is presented.

It is important to note that the cost of making buildings accessible, which is one important type of reasonable accommodation, will be covered in Chapter III. In balancing costs and benefits for the entire regulation the reader should be careful not to double count the costs of making buildings accessible. The cost of building accessibility should be added to the non-accessibility costs, and then this total cost should be compared to the sum of the benefits derived from Subparts B, C, and D (again being sure not to double count any benefits).

Benefits

There will be both social and pecuniary benefits from eliminating job discrimination in local educational agencies. Society in general, and the handicapped worker in particular, will obtain some social benefits from the elimination of employment discrimination. The fact that social benefits cannot be easily measured objectively does not make them any less significant; they should be considered when the overall balance is struck between costs and benefits.

Pecuniary benefits accrue in the form of increased earnings and employment stability for the disabled workers (which will be reflected in their greater contribution to the Gross National Product).

How great are these pecuniary benefits likely to be? Given the state of existing knowledge, there is no basis for anything more than an informed guess. We estimate that the regulation might affect about one million disabled workers. We also estimate that the annual earnings of partially workdisabled males might be as much as 18% lower on account of employment discrimination. Combining these two estimates yields an estimate of approximately $1 billion per year in benefits via the higher earnings capacity of handicapped workers.

For purposes of this analysis, the summary of benefits and costs uses the figure of $500 million as the likely benefits of the regulation. This represents half of the total difference in earnings associated with being handicapped for those likely to work for employers covered by Section 504 regulation. Halving the estimate provides a rough basis for the combined effects of (a) unmeasured differences in productivity not involving discrimination, and (b) the possibility that displacement of the non-handicapped will occur and reduce their earnings.

Costs associated with reasonable accommodation

Paragraph 84.12 of Subpart B requires local educational agencies to make reasonable outlays on whatever special resources are needed for full utilization of handicapped applicants. As noted above, probably the major source of cost increase associated with reasonable accommodation in employment—that of making buildings physically accessible—is covered in Chapter III. For most cases, the only other types of accommodations that are envisaged are those that involve little more than discarding stereotypes about what impact employing handicapped workers will have on the school district.

One of the most widespread of these myths is that employing handicapped workers will decrease safety performance and increase disability and life insurance rates. A number of studies have shown that this is not the case.

If a local educational agency has never employed a handicapped worker then the chances are it has not done any systematic thinking about the task content of its various job categories. It may appear at first that someone with a dramatic physical handicap (e.g., a totally blind person) could not perform the work at the productivity level of a non-handicapped person. However, many educational jobs involve primarily mental tasks and once the percent of sub-tasks that require the missing physical ability (sight, use of both hands, etc.) falls below a certain percentage, it is possible, and often simple, to restructure the job situation so that the handicapped worker can perform equally well as non-handicapped workers.

Experts in the area of vocational rehabilitation stress a general principle that explains some of the surprising patterns in the data on earning by type and severity of disability. The basic idea is that the variety of job situations in a modern economy combined with the great variety of forms that physical disabilities take, assures that there will be at least a few rewarding and remunerative jobs that can be very easily restructured for any physically handicapped individual. Data on the employment of veterans show that there is relatively high earnings and employment participation among even very severely handicapped veterans. This is some indirect evidence for the general principle. More direct evidence will not be presented. There have been a number of surveys that document what firms have done to accommodate handicapped workers. The initial experience of the Office of Federal Contract Compliance and Programs (OFCCP) with enforcing Section 503 is also reviewed. Finally, we present a detailed documentation of the types of jobs that have successfully adapted to accommodate totally blind individuals.

Survey studies. We present the findings of three surveys, one by the Civil Service Commission (CSC), one by the DuPont Company and the one cited above that was undertaken to help disabled Vietnam veterans with their employment problems.

In August 1970, the Office of Selective Placement of the Civil Service Commission completed a survey of their placement of severely handicapped individuals in the Federal government. The handicapped individuals studied did not include mildly or moderately handicapped individuals but only those individuals whose handicap was sufficiently severe to preclude their placement through regular competitive service procedures. The following description of the surveyed employees reveals that they constitute the group which is traditionally the hardest to place in employment and the one which would be expected to create the most severe problems in terms of the cost of accommodation:

> More than one-third of the appointees were deaf or had severe hearing

losses. Most of the deaf were also mute. Other disabilities commonly noted were blindness, upper and lower body impairments, and amputations. More than half of the appointees had multiple impairments.

Nevertheless, very little job restructuring or work-site modification was necessary to accommodate the limitations of these employees. In terms of job restructuring, 317 of the 397 persons placed required no accommodation, 62 required some (described by the respondents as "incidental"), and 18 did not respond. Thus, of the 397 who did respond, 80.5% or 4 out of 5 required no job restructuring at all.

In terms of modification of work-sites, 336 persons required no modification, 44 required some (primarily minor changes, such as adjustment of work benches), and 17 did not respond. Thus, of the 380 who did respond, 86.9% or 7 out of 8 required no work-site modification. The CSC report based on the survey concludes that ". . . contrary to the general assumption, the severely handicapped do not usually, or even often, require major alterations in a job situation. When changes are made, they were such incidental things as installing a wheelchair ramp at a building entrance, rearranging desks and file cabinets to improve mobility and accessibility, etc."

Another study was conducted at E. I. DuPont de Nemours and Company. The occupations of the employees studied and the range of their handicaps, as well as the results of the study, were described in an article published in *Alliance Review*. The relevant findings were that there was no increase in insurance costs and that the physical adjustment required were minimal, with most of the handicapped workers requiring no special work arrangements. In terms of safety, job performance measures, job stability and attendance record, the handicapped workers as a group scored higher than non-handicapped workers.

In the survey of disabled Vietnam Era veterans (which included a large fraction of severely disabled veterans) a question was asked each veteran about what special accommodations (if any) were made by their employer. Only 11% of the veterans who had held a job in 1973 reported that any special accommodation was made. Figure 10 presents a distribution of the accommodations reported by type of special arrangement. The authors of the study based on this survey conducted extensive content analysis of all the responses they received. They concluded, ". . . most of the special arrangements make minimal demands on, or entail minimal costs to the employer . . . even in cases where the employer provided special equipment, the cost seemed to be minimal."

OFCCP Experience with Section 503. OFCCP has the responsibility for enforcing non-discriminatory employment of handicapped individuals by all employers who receive contracts from the Federal government. As stated previously, Section 503 regulation is similar to Section 504, Subpart B regulation except that Section 503 requires that affirmative action be taken. It is generally agreed that affirmative action can imply a significantly higher level of extra effort than implied by the concept of reasonable accommodation. Thus, the use of the 503 experience as a guide to what will happen under 504 is clearly conservative in that 503 will, because of its affirmative action provision, lead to larger costs than will be necessary under 504.

Mr. Brigham of OFCCP provided detailed information on what the early

Figure 10

Categories of Special Job Arrangements Made by Employers and Percent of Veterans Reporting Arrangements in Each Category*

Special Job Arrangements	Percent	N
Flexibility of hours	18	56
Extra rest breaks	16	49
Assigned to appropriate job in the first place	16	49
Regular duties but no lifting	13	40
Change of duties or transfer of job	10	31
Special equipment	8	24
Work at own pace	7	22
Special parking	5	16
Help from supervisor or others	4	12
Miscellaneous	2	5

*Based on a content analysis of 304 randomly selected job arrangements reported by disabled veterans in response to the question, "Did your employer make arrangements so that you could work with your disability?" (For example, extra rest periods, special parking, special equipment for doing the work, change of job duties, help from supervisor.)

experience under Section 503 has been. With procedures recommending a sixty-day "cooling off" period during which a potential complaint is discussed between only the employer and the handicapped worker, Mr. Brigham reported that the large majority of complaints have been disposed of during this "cooling off" period without having required any hearings before Federal officials. Through 1975, a total of 331 complaints have not been resolved during the cooling off period and have reached the level of arbitration before OFCCP officials. It follows, therefore, that these 331 complaints represent predominantly serious situations. The average situation over all workers who initiate complaints will be made less serious and costly.

Mr. Brigham indicated that almost all of the difficult cases to date fall into two categories. One category involves disabilities caused by disease entities that have not obviously stabilized—cancer, diabetes, etc. Here the position of OFCCP has been that if the person is qualified at the present time then the burden of proof is on the employer to show that the costs of the unexpected recurrence of the disease entity (e.g., costs of providing a new worker with break-in training) are so high as to make the accommodation unreasonable. Mr. Brigham noted that the crucial factor in determining whether the cost imposed would be unreasonable is the size of the firm and the proportion of total employment cost that the extra cost would constitute.

The other category involves cases associated with emotional handicaps. How to define reasonable accommodation in these situations requires difficult judgments. A related issue is that of determining whether the complaining person really considered himself a handicapped person or if he is just using the handicap as a way of saving a job that he/she is being dismissed from on other grounds.

Jobs and accommodations for blind individuals. Since World War II there have been a number of very detailed surveys of the employment situations of totally blind veterans. Many studies of job restructuring aimed at opening up jobs for blind individuals are readily available. The most well known judicial decision on what constitutes reasonable accommodation also involved a blind individual. Thus, the information about adjustments required for people who are totally blind, which is a very severe disability, can be used to illustrate in detail what reasonable accommodation might entail in practice for local educational agencies.

The court case of Bevan v. N.Y. State Teachers Retirement System involved a blind teacher in upstate New York. The New York State education law contains a regulation that specifically forbids school administrators from laying off a teacher who goes blind as long as the handicap does not interfere with his ability to teach. In his argument, the judge reasoned that blindness in and of itself does not impair the faculties required to be an effective teacher (e.g., ability to organize material for presentation, or present that material orally before the class), hence he ruled that the law required the school system to supply the teacher with whatever special resources were necessary to carry out ancillary functions (e.g., paper grading and calling on students who raise their hands).

What does the extra cost of employing a blind teacher actually amount to in practice? In the school year 1968-69 there were 334 blind teachers working in elementary and secondary schools in the United States. Huntington did a study based on questionnaire and personal interviews with some of these teachers and with the school administrators in the systems where they worked. He questioned administrators on eight potential problem areas: (a) lunchroom supervision, (b) test administration, (c) study hall supervision, (d) chaperoning student activities, (e) use of visual aids, (f) fire drills, (g) keeping written records, and (h) discipline. For all the categories, Huntington found that either the blind teacher could do what appeared at first to require sight (e.g., lead children out of the building at fire drills), or that compensating substitutions could be made between the different categories (e.g., taking on more monitoring duties like study hall and dances instead of lunchroom supervision). Discipline turned out not to be the problem that had been expected. However, Huntington does mention the caveat that there is still some disagreement about the feasibility of blind teachers in elementary schools. The amounts of extra resources that the average blind teacher requires were very minor—a braille typewriter and a cassette tape recorder for keeping records and the occasional use of an honor student to help proctor examinations and then read the answers into a tape recorder.

In sum, Huntington's analysis suggests that the only area of controversy in deciding what constitutes reasonable accommodation for blind teachers is the question of the age of the students. Clearly the issues of discipline and effective pedagogy (Is it important educationally for the teacher to be able to see the young child's reaction?) could be important at the lower elementary grade levels. However, Huntington's analysis also shows that there will be no cost problems in enforcing reasonable accommodation for blind teachers at the secondary and college level.

Figure 11 shows how a sample of totally blind veterans were distributed by types of jobs. The very uneven distribution of the totally blind by type of work suggests that the enforcement of reasonable accommodation will have to be very flexible—not all jobs can be easily adapted to lack of sight although the range of possibilities that turns up in practice is truly surprising.

Figure 11

Distribution of Jobs of 338 Totally Blind Veterans Among Dot Part IV Classifications
(Percent Distribution)

		Percent
Professional, Technical, and Managerial Work (147)		37.9%
Musical work (4)	2.7%	
Literary work (7)	4.7	
Public service work (27)	18.3	
Technical work (17)	11.5	
Managerial work (92)	62.5	
	100.0	
Clerical and Sales Work (54)		13.9
Recording work (4)	7.4%	
General clerical work (3)	5.5	
Public contact work (47)	87.0	
	100.0	
General public contact (15)		
Selling (32)		
Service Work (6)		1.5
Farming (48)		12.3
General farming (18)	37.5%	
Animal care (28)	58.3	
Fruit farming and gardening (2)	4.1	
	100.0	
Mechanical Work (37)		9.5
Machine trades (8)	21.6%	
Store or glass machining (1)		
Mechanical repairing (7)		
Crafts (29)	78.3	
	100.0	
Electrical repairing (8)		
Bench work (11)		
Inspecting and testing (2)		
Photographic work (8)		
Manual Work (96)		24.7
Observational work (5)	5.2%	
Manipulative work (70)	72.9	
Benchwork (Assembled and related) (45)		
Machine Operating, Manipulative (25)		
Elemental work (21)	21.8	
	100.0	100.0

Source: *Occupations of Totally Blinded . . ., Ibid.*, p. 6.

The study based on this survey lists in detail the arrangements and accommodations surrounding each of the 388 job situations. It is difficult to summarize this material in that the specific types of minor devices, task restructuring and use of sighted individuals is so diverse. In the professional public service and managerial areas the part-time assistance of a graduate student (or other secondary worker—wife, elderly part-time worker, etc.) is usually the only extra resource required (when any are required at all). In the employment and clerical field the accommodation usually involves only minor job restructuring to allow the blind clerk or secretary to specialize in those parts of the office information network that do not require immediate sight (e.g., handling information received over the phone and stored in dictaphones as opposed to processing written information left in in-boxes that require immediate response).

Recent developments in job restructuring technology suggest that the clerical area is going to become a more important source of employment for blind individuals. The general area is called "information service processing" and includes such jobs as central office clerical positions and data processing positions.

Summary of costs. For purposes of this analysis, the summary of benefits and costs uses the figure of $50 million in costs for reasonable accommodation in employment. We estimate that perhaps a million disabled workers would be covered by Subpart B. Even if we assume that the reasonable accommodation provision would result in an expenditure of $100 per year on one-half of them (which is probably an overestimate of numbers that would require special resources) that would only come to $50 million. This amount corresponds to about one-half of one percent of costs for these employees and perhaps one-fortieth of one percent of total compensation of all employment covered by the regulation.

Modification recommendations for staffing procedures and practices

The job analysis profile includes: (a) basic descriptive data, including the job that was analyzed, date of analysis, job analyst's name, address, and telephone number, job analysis population, sample, and sample size, (b) list of competencies by category (rank ordered), and (c) compilation sheet delineating median scores for specific job analysis variables/worker competencies. Combined with the narrative report, the job analyst can make specific recommendations concerning: (a) job-related accommodations needed to provide qualified handicapped individuals with appropriate employment opportunities, and (b) the degree of compliance between the local educational agency's personnel staffing process and Section 504, Subpart B regulation. Consulting with administrative decision-makers and handicapped individuals involved in personnel staffing, the job analyst or self-evaluation coordinator can either: (a) examine possible accommodations for a specific job within a specific educational setting (e.g., the assistant principals position at Dunbar Elementary School) using information obtained from the study, or (b) examine possible accommodations for a generic category applicable to a variety of educational settings (e.g., eight elementary school teachers) also using information obtained from the study.

No set accommodation criteria can be established. Individual handicapping conditions (e.g., deaf or blind) may require different forms of accommodation. Furthermore, essential job-related competencies, individual worker physical, affective, and cognitive traits, and the unique characteristics of each work setting will necessitate that, whenever possible, reasonable accommodation should be approached on a case-by-case basis. For example, can the essential job analysis variables/worker competencies delineated for the assistant principals position at Dunbar Elementary School be modified to accommodate a blind applicant? The answer to this question would not only require examining the relationship between job analysis variables/worker competencies and the individual handicapped applicant, but also require examining the necessary staff and facility accommodations that will have to be made at Dunbar Elementary School.

In conclusion, O'Neill's analysis of costs, benefits, and economic impact suggests that enforcement of reasonable accommodation will not result in any significant cost increase for local educational agencies. Most of the Labor Department cases have involved no financial outlay or, at most, a few hundred dollars. However, there are situations in which accommodation would, except for very large local educational agencies, require significant financial outlays, and/or risks and disruptions, and the present working of the regulation gives no precise guidance as how to define what accommodations are reasonable. This suggests that thought should be given to alternative ways of working the provision. One possible approach would be to define reasonableness as a percent of per employee costs. A local educational agency might consider setting maximum percent per employee costs for a variety of work positions. These figures could be set after: (a) determining, through a job analysis study, what accommodations will be necessary for a variety of work positions, and (b) in consultation with currently employed handicapped individuals and interested individuals and groups. While no completely satisfactory solution has yet been developed, this approach would provide an important starting point.

Phase VI: Evaluation

Phase VI concerns ascertaining the effectiveness of the self-evaluation program including the job analysis study and architectural barriers discrepancy analysis. There are five areas of evaluation that need to be identified and used by the self-evaluation coordinator: (a) systems assessment, (b) program planning, (c) program implementation, (d) program improvement, and (e) program certification. These five areas represent attempts to provide evaluation information to satisfy unique decision categories. In general, these five areas of evaluation are necessary: (a) to provide information for decisions about future school system modifications necessary to comply with Section 504 regulation, (b) to provide information to assist in the selection of particular program modifications likely to be effective in meeting specific employment, program accessibility, and educational needs, (c) to provide information relative to the extent to which a self-evaluation program has been introduced in the manner in which it was intended and to the individuals and groups for which it was intended, (d) to provide information during the course of a self-evaluation program about the manner in which the program is functioning, objectives being achieved, and what anticipated and unanticipated outcomes are produced, and (f) to provide information that can be used by administrative decision-makers in making judgments concerning the worth of the self-evaluation program and its potential generalizability to other related situations. Regardless of the specific evaluation technique used (e.g., PPBS, PERT, MBO, or critical path), the self-evaluation coordinator will need information pertaining to each of these five areas to ascertain the effectiveness of the self-evaluation program.

To summarize, the author examined in Chapter II the legislative and judicial development of Section 504 concepts, specific regulatory requirements, and organizational structure and operation issues relative to the staffing process. In delineating a generic self-evaluation model appropriate for meeting Section 504 requirements, the author emphasized a job analysis approach in examining a local educational agency's employment practices and procedures.

Chapter III

Program Accessability

Subpart C of Section 504 regulation requires recipients of Department of Health, Education and Welfare financial assistance to ensure that no qualified handicapped individual is denied or excluded from participating in or benefiting from any program or activity because a recipient's facilities are inaccessible to handicapped individuals. Like Subpart B, Subpart C is applicable to *all* recipients of Department of Health, Education and Welfare financial assistance, including state, intermediate, and local educational agencies. Subpart C regulation concerns both existing facilities and new construction.

In its November 1974 first report to the Congress, the Architectural and Transportation Barriers Compliance Board succinctly summarized the accessability problems of handicapped individuals.

> Approximately 22 million people, or 10 percent of the entire population in the United States have physical impairments which restrict them from normal daily activities. For the most part, they are a hidden population, isolated in a household environment and restricted from contributing their talents as active members of the community. One of the major obstacles to their participation in societal endeavors is the physical design of our man-made environment. The transportation systems, buildings, and facilities that are an integral part of our urban environments are designed and built to accommodate only a portion of its residents—the physically unimpaired.[1]

In concert with Subpart C of Section 504 regulation, Public Law 94-142, The Education For All Handicapped Children Act, requires public agencies that operate in states which receive payments under Part B of the Education of the Handicapped Act (Public Law 93-380) to ensure that: (a) to the maximum extent appropriate, handicapped children are educated with children who are not handicapped, and (b) that special classes, separate schooling or other removal of handicapped children from the regular educational environment occurs only when the nature or severity of the handicap is such that education in regular classes with the use of supplementary aids and services cannot be achieved satisfactorily. Furthermore, each public agency must ensure that a continuum of alternative placements is available to meet the needs of handicapped children for special education and related services. This continuum of alternative placements includes instruction in regular classes, special classes, special schools, home instruction, and instruction in hospitals and institutions. Supplementary services such as resource room or itinerant instruction should be provided in conjunction with regular class placement. Therefore, for the delivery of educational services, P.L. 94-142 addresses two important issues. First, the needs of the handicapped child should determine what direct and support services are provided, and in which educational setting. Second, P.L. 94-142 does not recognize physical facility inaccessability as a legal or ethical exemption for providing educational services to a handicapped child in a specific educational setting.

Two basic assumptions the author proposes are:
- To successfully implement Section 504 program accessibility requirements, public school personnel must understand the role of discrepancy analysis in evaluating program accessibility; and
- The procedures and techniques employed in an architectural barriers discrepancy analysis are not only appropriate for meeting Subpart C program accessibility requirements, but appropriate for the determination of physical accessibility to the work setting for qualified handicapped workers.

The remaining portion of Chapter III examines:
- The developmental history of Section 504, Subpart C program accessibility regulation, including (a) legislative history, and (b) judicial history;
- Specific regulatory requirements, including (a) regulation applicable to existing facilities, and (b) regulation applicable to new construction; and
- Program accessibility issues relative with the structure and operation of local educational agencies, including (a) implementation of the self-evaluation design, with emphasis on an architectural barriers discrepancy analysis, and (b) modifying current program accessibility, with emphasis on modifying existing facilities and new construction.

Developmental History of Section 504 Regulation: Legislative History[2]

The Vocational Rehabilitation Act, amended in 1965 to expand the public program for rehabilitating the handicapped, authorized the National Commission on Architectural Barriers. The Commission grew out of a congressional mandate to eliminate architectural barriers and to establish plans for further congressional action. This congressional mandate climaxed the efforts of the public and nonprofit groups that had worked to secure voluntary compliance with the *American National Standard Specifications for Making Buildings and Facilities Accessible to, and Usable by, the Physically Handicapped.*[3]

The ANSI standard was developed by the President's Committee on

Employment of the Handicapped, the National Society for Crippled Children and Adults, and various Federal and private agencies. It was field tested by disabled students from the University of Illinois. On October 31, 1961, the American National Standards Institute, established to coordinate the development of voluntary national standards, issued the *ANSI Standard.* The *Standard* was distributed throughout the United States by various organizations, including the National Easter Seal Society for Crippled Children and Adults.

By 1965, 24 states had taken some kind of legislative action to eliminate architectural barriers in public buildings. Much of the legislation, however, was discretionary and not sufficiently comprehensive in coverage. With no concerted local effort to develop and activate accessibility programs, few public buildings were being constructed barrier free. Furthermore, at the Federal level, no executive order had been issued to ensure elimination of barriers in the design and construction of Federally assisted projects.

In 1967 the National Commission on Architectural Barriers recommended to the Congress legislation requiring accessibility in all buildings leased or owned by the government or constructed with Federal funds. On August 12, 1968, the Congress enacted Public Law 90-480, known as the Architectural Barriers Act of 1968. The Act's purpose was to ensure that certain Federally funded buildings were designed and constructed to be accessible to the physically handicapped. Included in P.L. 90-480 were Federally financed buildings in which a physically handicapped individual might live or work and buildings intended for public use. Privately owned residential structures and those on military installations were specifically excluded.

Sections 2, 3, and 4 of the Architectural Barriers Act authorized the Director of the General Services Administration (GSA) and the Secretaries of Housing and Urban Development (HUD) and Defense (DOD), in consultation with the Secretary of Health, Education and Welfare (HEW), to prescribe standards for the design, construction, and alteration of buildings. In practice, GSA, DOD, HUD, and HEW followed the ANSI *Standard.*

Section 6 of the Architectural Barriers Act authorized applicable Federal agencies to: (a) make whatever surveys and investigations deemed necessary to ensure compliance with the ANSI Standard, and (b) modify or waive the ANSI standards on a case-by-case basis upon application by the director of the agency involved. In general, the Architectural Barriers Act brought the Federal government to the level of legislative initiative already reached by 34 states. Public Law 91-205, approved March 5, 1970, amended the Architectural Barriers Act to make it applicable to the Washington, D.C. Metro subway facilities (now under construction).

Section 502 of the Rehabilitation Act of 1973, enacted on September 26, 1973 created an Architectural and Transportation Barriers Compliance Board. The Board's functions include:

- Ensuring compliance with the ANSI *Standards* prescribed by GSA, DOD, and HUD pursuant to the Architectural Barriers Act;
- Initiating investigations on the nature of architectural, transportation,

and attitudinal barriers confronting the handicapped, particularly with respect to public buildings and monuments, parks and parklands, public transportation systems, and residential and institutional housing;
- Considering the housing needs of the handicapped;
- Determining how and to what extent transportation barriers impede the mobility of the handicapped and considering ways in which their travel expenses to and from work can be met or subsidized;
- Determining the actions being taken by other governmental units and public and nonprofit agencies, and preparing proposals for consolidating the efforts of agencies, organizations, and groups whose cooperation is essential for effective and comprehensive action;
- Conducting investigations, holding public hearings, and issuing such orders as it deems necessary to ensure compliance with the Rehabilitation Act's provisions; and
- Making recommendations to the President and to the Congress for administration and legislation as deemed necessary or desirable to eliminate architectural, transportation, and attitudinal barriers to the handicapped.

The Architectural and Transportation Barriers Compliance Board was established as an independent body composed initially of eight agencies: (a) Department of Health, Education and Welfare, (b) Housing and Urban Development, (c) General Services Administration, (d) Department of the Interior, (e) Department of Labor, (f) Department of Transportation, (g) Veterans Administration, and (h) Postal Service. No single agency had administrative responsibility for operation. On December 7, 1974, Section 502 was amended by Section III of the Rehabilitation Act Amendments of 1974 to:
- Make the Department of Defense a board member;
- Make the Secretary of HEW (or his designee) Chairman of the Board;
- Give the Board authority to appoint a consumer's advisory panel, a majority of whose members would be handicapped, to give the Board guidance, advice, and recommendations; and
- Give the Board authority to withhold or suspend Federal funds to any building found not to be in compliance with standards prescribed pursuant to the Architectural Barriers Act, as amended.

By 1974, all 50 states and the District of Columbia had, through legislation, executive directives, or building codes, required the elimination of architectural barriers in public buildings.

Developmental History of Section 504 Regulation: Judicial History[4]

With respect to public buildings, Federal law requires that all new Federal and Federally assisted facilities designed for public use be readily accessible; however, with the exception of Section 504 regulation, there are few provisions for existing structures. State statutes addressing the problem of architectural barriers also generally ignore the need for modifications of existing buildings. It should be noted that the Supreme Court long has recognized that citizens have the right to come to their "seats of government" to transact business and petition for redress of grievances. This freedom to petition is protected by the First Amendment and applies to all branches of government, including the administrative agencies.

Since the physical barriers which impede the handicapped individual's access generally exist because of poor planning choices and serve no useful purpose, they may be attacked as unreasonable and discriminatory. States have the alternative when building facilities to use designs which would make facilities fully accessible at similar cost. By an official choice of construction, a state may possibly infringe upon the rights of handicapped persons; therefore, the state has a duty to eliminate all such impediments to the free exercise by handicapped individuals of their rights. The courts will tend to order building modifications, costly or otherwise, when Bill of Rights freedoms are involved.

In Washington Urban League v. Washington Metropolitan Area Transit Authority (1973), Judge William Jones enjoined the Washington Metro Subway System from operating commercially until it was made accessible to physically handicapped persons by the installation of vertical elevators. Since the Metro case centered on a question of statutory interpretation, the defendant's arguments and actions, interpreting handicapped persons out of the transportation system, are instructive as to the price handicapped citizens have had to pay for reliance on legislative measures to achieve reform and augment services. The history of discrimination in generic programs leading to specialized legislation to provide for handicapped persons, requiring specialized funding, which may or may not be provided, has led to some peculiar attitudes and assumptions relating to rights of handicapped persons under statute.

In reviewing implementation of state statutes, it is possible to derive two widely practiced rules of construction which, until recently, have gone unchallenged. First, that general laws providing benefits and protection to all citizens implicitly exclude handicapped persons. Second, that mandatory language in specialized legislation is something less than mandatory when applied to handicapped persons.

Architectural barriers legislation is but another example. While provisions vary from state to state, coverage is generally limited to new public buildings, enforcement is diffuse and weak, and the statutes are riddled with waiver clauses. Thus, it is important for local educational agencies to establish that these statutes are in no way pre-emptive—that they do not define the limits of right to access to public buildings and accommodations.

The right to travel and to use the instrumentalities of interstate commerce are fundamental rights under the Constitution. The issue here is how this right and other First Amendment rights affect transportation of handicapped individuals on intercity buses, rail, airplanes, and other forms or instrumentalities of transportation. Lawsuits aimed at achieving actual accessibility in public transportation, especially for persons in wheelchairs, have been brought in New

York, Washington, California, Alabama, Wisconsin, Michigan, and Maryland. Thus far the courts have not recognized a right to actual access by persons who use wheelchairs.

Another instance in which a Federal agency has not made adequate provision for the disabled through its rulemaking authority is found in the airline situation. At the present time the Federal Aviation Agency (FAA) has yet to issue permanent provisions which impose a duty on all interstate airlines to serve the severely disabled. Therefore, airlines' pilots and officers have had extensive discretion in determining whether to allow the disabled on airplanes. The theory behind this discretion is that disabled are most likely to be injured in a crash or will take up valuable time of the flight personnel in an emergency. The first theory disregards the disabled person's own willingness to take the risk of such danger. Each airline has instituted its own policy in this regard.

In terms of future litigation the newly proposed Federal regulations may not improve the situation greatly. Under the proposed regulations, only the same number of severely disabled persons are permitted on each flight as there are emergency exits, and only one person confined to a litter is permitted per flight. The handicapped person is not allowed to sit in the seat nearest any of the exits. Another drawback of the proposed regulation is the definition of a handicapped person as "a person who may need the assistance of another person to expeditiously move to an exit in the event of an emergency evacuation." As stated by Senator Tunney, this definition is "so vague and general that anyone from one's grandmother to a skier with a sprained ankle could be classed as handicapped."

Delineation of Specific Regulatory Requirements[5]

There is one general requirement of the Section 504 regulation concerning program accessibility. This general requirement is: no qualified handicapped person shall, because a recipient's facilities are inaccessible to or unusable by handicapped persons, be denied the benefits of, be excluded from participation in, or otherwise be subjected to discrimination under any program or activity receiving Federal financial assistance. Specifically, this general requirement applies to a school district's existing facilities and new construction.

Existing facilities

Paragraph 84.22(a) of the regulation specifies that a recipient of Federal financial assistance must operate each program or activity so that, when viewed in its entirety, such a program or activity is readily accessible to handicapped individuals. This paragraph does not require a school district to make each of its existing facilities or every part of a facility accessible to and usable by handicapped individuals. However, while a public school district need not make each of its buildings completely accessible, it may not make only one facility or part of a facility accessible if the result is to segregate handicapped students in a single setting. A school district may comply with the requirements of Paragraph 84.22(a) through such means as: (a) redesigning of equipment, (b) reassignment of classes or other services to accessible buildings, (c) assignment of aides to beneficiaries, (d) home visits, (e) delivery of services at alternate accessible sites, and (f) altering existing facilities or constructing new facilities. A school district is not required to make structural changes in existing facilities where other methods are effective in achieving compliance with Paragraph 84.22(a). In choosing among available methods, a school district must give priority to those methods that offer programs and activities to handicapped individuals in the most integrated educational employment setting appropriate.

While local educational agencies should have complied with the requirement of Paragraph 84.22 (a) within sixty days of the regulation's effective date (May 4, 1977), where structural changes in facilities are necessary, such changes should be made before May 4, 1980. In the event that structural changes to facilities are necessary, a local educational agency must develop, within six months of the regulation's effective date (May 4, 1977), a transition plan that delineates necessary steps to complete such changes. This transition plan should be developed with the assistance of interested persons, including handicapped individuals or organizations representing handicapped individuals. Furthermore, a copy of the transition plan must be made available for public inspection.

At a minimum, the transition plan must include:
- An identification of physical obstacles in the school district's facilities that limit the accessibility of its program or activity to handicapped individuals;
- A detailed description of the methods that will be used to make the facilities accessible;
- A specification of the schedule for taking the steps necessary to achieve full program accessibility and, if the time period of the transition plan is longer than one year, an identification of steps that will be taken during each year of the transition period; and
- An identification of the person responsible for implementing the plan.

And finally, the local educational agency must adopt and implement procedures to ensure that interested individuals, including persons with impaired vision or hearing, can obtain information as to the existence and location of services, activities, and facilities that are accessible to and usable by handicapped individuals.

New construction

Paragraph 84.23(a) of the regulation specifies that a recipient of Federal financial assistance must ensure that each new facility must be designed and constructed in such a manner that the facility (or part of the facility) is readily accessible to and usable by handicapped individuals. This requirement pertains only to construction commenced after the effective date of Subpart C (May 4, 1977). Also, each facility (or part of the facility) which is altered after the effective date in a manner that affects or could affect the usability of the facility by handicapped individuals, must be altered in such a manner that the altered facility is readily accessible and usable to such individuals. For example, if a doorway or wall is being altered, then the door or other wall opening must be made wide enough to accommodate wheelchairs. The Department of Health, Education and Welfare will allow for the occasional case in which the nature of an existing facility is such as to make it impractical or prohibitively expensive to renovate the building in a manner that results in its being entirely barrier-free. In all such cases, however, the alteration must provide the maximum amount of physical accessibility feasible.

As a minimum requirement, the design, construction, or alteration of facilities should be in conformance with the *American National Standard Specifications for Making Buildings and Facilities Accessible to, and Usable by, the Physically Handicapped,* published by the American National Standards Institute, Inc. Departures from particular ANSI Standards by the use of other methods is appropriate when it is clearly evident that equivalent facility accessibility is provided.

Program Accessibility Issues Relative to the Structure and Operation of Local Educational Agencies

Repeating what was stated in Chapter II, the Office for Civil Rights of the Department of Health, Education and Welfare specifies that three types of organizational action are required to comply with Section 504 regulation. These actions are: (a) remedial action, (b) voluntary action, and (c) self-evaluation. If the local educational agency has discriminated against individuals on the basis of handicap in violation of Section 504, the local educational agency must take such remedial action as the Director of the Office for Civil Rights deems necessary to overcome the effects of the discrimination. Furthermore a local educational agency may take voluntary action, in addition to any remedial action that is required, to overcome the effects of conditions that resulted in limited participation in the local district's programs or activities by qualified handicapped individuals. However, it is essential that districts develop a specific self-evaluation plan, and district policies and procedures for its implementation.

As presented previously, Figure 12 delineates the necessary conceptual components for planning, conducting, and analyzing a self-evaluation design.

In the remaining portion of Chapter III, we will examine those self-evaluation components applicable to local educational agency program accessibility. Phases I through III were examined in Chapter II. The program accessibility requirements of Subpart C do not necessitate alternating these phases. Therefore, Chapter III will emphasize:

Figure 12
Conceptual Components for a Self-Evaluation Design

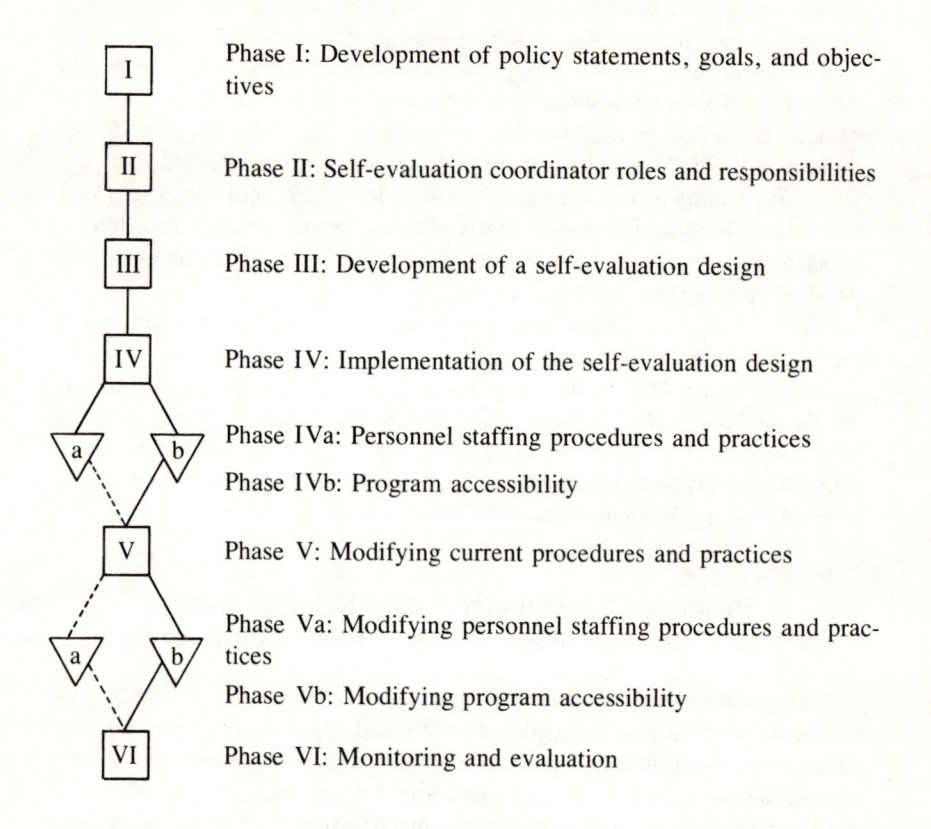

I — Phase I: Development of policy statements, goals, and objectives

II — Phase II: Self-evaluation coordinator roles and responsibilities

III — Phase III: Development of a self-evaluation design

IV — Phase IV: Implementation of the self-evaluation design

a / b — Phase IVa: Personnel staffing procedures and practices
Phase IVb: Program accessibility

V — Phase V: Modifying current procedures and practices

a / b — Phase Va: Modifying personnel staffing procedures and practices
Phase Vb: Modifying program accessibility

VI — Phase VI: Monitoring and evaluation

- Phase IVb: Implemention of the self-evaluation design, including an architectural barriers discrepancy analysis;
- Phase Vb: Modifying program accessibility, including modification of physical accessibility barriers for qualified handicapped workers and program participants; and
- Phase VI: Monitoring and evaluation.

To comply with Section 504, Subpart C program accessibility requirements, the self-evaluation coordinator will need to delineate the discrepancy between current physical accessibility to the districts facilities for program participants and qualified handicapped workers, and applicable Section 504, Subpart B and C regulation. And to successfully delineate the discrepancy between current program accessibility and Section 504, Subpart B and C regulation requirements, the self-evaluation coordinator must understand the role of discrepancy analysis.

Discrepancy analysis. Discrepancy analysis is "the comparison of what is, a performance (P), to an expectation of what should be, a standard (S)."[6] As described by Yavorsky,

> If a difference is found to exist between the standard and the performance, this difference is known as a discrepancy (D). Discrepancies may be positive, where performance exceeds the standard, or negative, where performance is less than the standard. Whereas positive discrepancies are usually welcome, negative discrepancies generally cause concern. Negative discrepancies may be resolved in three ways: an unrealistic standard may be reformulated or redesigned; management may exert greater control over performance; or, if the discrepancy is unmanageable, a program may be terminated.[7]

For this handbook, the American National Standard Institute's *Specifications For Making Buildings and Facilities Accessible to, and Usable by, the Physically Handicapped* will comprise the standard by which a district's program accessibility "performance" can be compared (See Appendix A). The results of the architectural barriers discrepancy analysis should be used: (a) to modify physical barriers impeding qualified handicapped workers from being employed or successfully fulfilling job responsibilities once employed, and (b) to modify physical barriers impeding handicapped individuals from successfully participating in a district's programs and activities. Both results can be obtained from the same architectural barriers discrepancy analysis.

In general, once the local educational agency accepts a program accessibility standard (e.g., ANSI *Standards*), the discrepancy analysis will usually involve: (a) observing the existence or nonexistence of specific architectural specifications, and (b) questioning/interviewing interested professionals and citizens as to planning and implementing modifications in program accessibility.

Conceptual delineation of architectural barriers discrepancy analysis. This portion of Chapter III describes planning, conducting, and analyzing procedures that can be followed by the self-evaluation coordinator in conducting an architectural barriers discrepancy analysis (Phase IVb: Implementation of the self-evaluation design). Similar to the techniques employed with the job analysis, the techniques used will secure detailed, valid, and authoritative architectural barriers information. The basic discrepancy analysis approach described is a combination of the three data gathering techniques used with the job analysis: (a) observation, (b) questioning/interviewing, and (c) measurement. Delineated in Figure 13 are the specific planning, conducting, and analyzing components of a discrepancy and analysis.

The planning component of the architectural barriers discrepancy analysis involves nine decision steps. These include:
- Determining the architectural barriers discrepancy analysis to be conducted;
- Determining who will conduct the architectural barriers discrepancy analysis;

Figure 13

The Planning, Conducting, and Analyzing Components of a Discrepancy Analysis

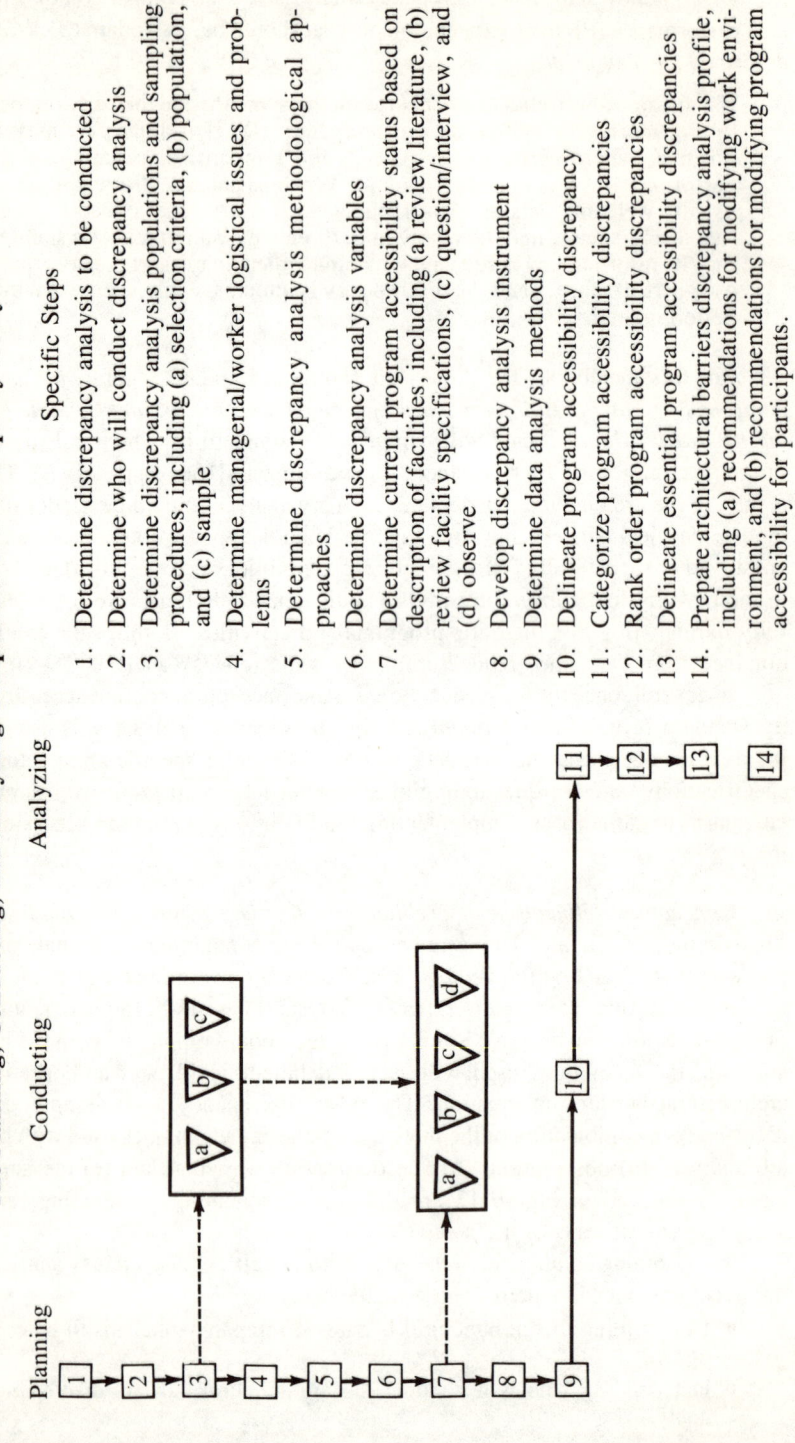

		Specific Steps
Planning		1. Determine discrepancy analysis to be conducted
		2. Determine who will conduct discrepancy analysis
Conducting		3. Determine discrepancy analysis populations and sampling procedures, including (a) selection criteria, (b) population, and (c) sample
		4. Determine managerial/worker logistical issues and problems
		5. Determine discrepancy analysis methodological approaches
		6. Determine discrepancy analysis variables
		7. Determine current program accessibility status based on description of facilities, including (a) review literature, (b) review facility specifications, (c) question/interview, and (d) observe
Analyzing		8. Develop discrepancy analysis instrument
		9. Determine data analysis methods
		10. Delineate program accessibility discrepancy
		11. Categorize program accessibility discrepancies
		12. Rank order program accessibility discrepancies
		13. Delineate essential program accessibility discrepancies
		14. Prepare architectural barriers discrepancy analysis profile, including (a) recommendations for modifying work environment, and (b) recommendations for modifying program accessibility for participants.

- Determining the architectural barriers discrepancy analysis populations and sampling procedures;
- Determining managerial/worker logistical issues and problems;
- Determining the architectural barriers discrepancy analysis methodological approaches;
- Determining the architectural barriers discrepancy analysis variables;
- Determining current program accessibility status based on description of facilities;
- Developing the architectural barriers discrepancy analysis instrument; and
- Determining the data analysis methods.

An examination of each of these nine planning components follows.

In determining the architectural barriers discrepancy analysis to be conducted, there are two fundamental questions that need to be addressed by the self-evaluation coordinator:

- Is the discrepancy analysis concerned with a specific educational facility (e.g., Dunbar Elementary School), or concerned with a generic category of facilities (e.g., all elementary schools in the district)?
- To whom are the results of the discrepancy analysis to be delivered (e.g., the principal of Dunbar Elementary School or the Assistant Superintendent of Maintenance for the district).

In determining who will conduct the architectural barriers discrepancy analysis, there are five fundamental questions that need to be addressed by the self-evaluation coordinator:

- Should the architectural barriers discrepancy analysis be conducted by personnel employed by the local educational agency or should services be contracted through an institution of higher learning, state department of education, intermediate administrative unit, or regional educational agency?
- Is it feasible for the self-evaluation coordinator to conduct the architectural barriers discrepancy analysis?
- What are the professional competencies necessary to conduct an architectural barriers discrepancy analysis?
- Are there social, political, or economical restrictions that will limit the range of individuals who conduct the architectural barriers discrepancy analysis?
- Who has the legal authority to negotiate for the services of an architectural barriers discrepancy analyst?

In determining the architectural barriers discrepancy analysis populations and sampling procedures, there are nine fundamental questions that need to be addressed by the self-evaluation coordinator:

- How does the selection of the architectural barriers discrepancy analysis to be conducted delimit the population of educational and non-educational facilities to be used?
- Which educational and non-educational facilities comprise the universe of all relevant sites to be studied or utilized in the study?

- Will it be necessary to analyze all of the district's educational and non-educational facilities, or will a sample of facilities provide adequate planning information?
- How are the educational and non-educational facilities selected and what are the identifiable characteristics of each facility?
- If the architectural barriers discrepancy analysis concerns a specific facility, who are those individuals or groups that should participate in the discrepancy analysis?
- If the architectural barriers discrepancy analysis concerns a generic facility category, who are those individuals or groups that should participate in the discrepancy analysis?
- How should these individuals or groups participate, and who determines whether or not these individuals or groups do participate?
- What "weight" is to be given to these other individual's or group's descriptions, judgments, and opinions concerning a specific facility or generic facility category?
- If a sampling process is employed, what financial and logistical problems are involved?

In determining the managerial/worker logistical issues and problems in conducting the architectural barriers discrepancy analysis, there are six fundamental questions that need to be addressed by the self-evaluation coordinator:
- How much will the architectural barriers discrepancy analysis cost?
- What local or state funds are available for use by the school system and the analyst?
- How cooperative will the individuals and groups involved in the study be in terms of completing the study?
- What are the political and social restraints placed on the analyst?
- What are the resource requirements necessary for conducting the architectural barriers discrepancy analysis?
- Are there local or state policies, regulations, or laws that can restrict the activities of the architectural barriers discrepancy analysis?

In determining the architectural barriers discrepancy analysis methodological approaches, the author suggests that the techniques used with the job analysis are appropriate for the discrepancy analysis. Therefore, the techniques of (a) observation, (b) questioning/interviewing, and (c) measurement can be used with the discrepancy analysis. The recommendations of Fox concerning the sequence of steps in applying both the observation and questioning/interviewing techniques can be used with the architectural barriers discrepancy analysis.

Concerning the conceptual delineation of techniques for questioning as a function of the analyst/respondent interaction and the response format (Figure 8), the author recommends that the totally structured impersonal or mixed format be used; therefore, checklist or structured questionnaire. This recommendation pertains to a specific building site or facility as well as a generic facility category.

When appropriate, the architectural barriers discrepancy analyst should question/interview program participants (including handicapped participants), educational personnel (e.g., teachers and administrators), and non-educational personnel (e.g., custodial and maintenance personnel). Specific questions and/or interview topics should concern: (a) program accessibility problems, (b) accommodations that have been made in the past for handicapped individuals, and (c) recommendations and suggestions made by program participants, educational personnel, and non-educational personnel.

With the observation method the analyst is basically concerned with a straightforward description of facility specifications in accordance with the ANSI *Standard* or appropriate state or local building code substitute. The same individuals involved in the observation of the job analysis can be employed to gather data for the architectural barriers discrepancy analysis.

In determining the architectural barriers discrepancy analysis variables to be included in the study, there are two fundamental questions that need to be addressed by the self-evaluation coordinator:

- Who determines the architectural barriers variables to be included in the study?
- Is the American National Institute's architectural *Standards* inclusive of all pertinent architectural variables?

Although the ANSI *Standards* provide the *minimum* requirements to comply with Section 504, Subpart C regulation, other modifications may be necessary to provide appropriate accommodation to qualified handicapped workers or meet the unique needs of handicapped students in the least restrictive environment. Therefore, the author recommends that the architectural barriers discrepancy analyst or self-evaluation coordinator develop facility standards that provide for: (a) maximum program participation by handicapped individuals, and (b) maximum accommodation in the work setting for qualified handicapped workers.

Regardless of the standard used, the discrepancy analysis should delineate at least seven salient categories of architectural variables. The seven categories are:

- Access to the classroom, including (a) parking lots, (b) walks and curbs, (c) ramps, (d) stairs and rails, (e) entrances and doors, (f) elevators, and (g) corridors and floors;
- Classroom facilities and materials, including (a) furniture and materials by type of handicap, and (b) general ideas for accessible classroom furniture;
- Play spaces;
- Sanitary facilities;
- Other facilities, including (a) auditoriums, (b) dining halls, (c) laboratories, (d) libraries, and (e) water fountains;
- Controls and warning signals; and
- Telephones.

Derived from the Educational Research Services document *Barrier-Free School Facilities for Handicapped Students,*[8] a series of questions can be asked concerning each of these variable categories. While these questions do not pertain to all pertinent architectural barriers, the reader can better ascertain the level of specificity needed to adequately determine whether facilities are barrier free.

Relative to parking lots:
- Are spaces that are accessible and approximate to the facility set aside and identified for use by individuals with disabilities?
- Are these parking spaces open on one side, allowing room for individuals in wheelchairs or individuals on braces and crutches to get in and out of an automobile onto a level surface?
- When placed between two conventional diagonal or head-on parking spaces, are the special parking spaces 12 feet across?
- Are individuals in wheelchairs and individuals using braces or crutches compelled to wheel or walk behind parked cars?
- Is the distribution of parking spaces for use by the disabled in accordance with the frequency and persistency of parking needs?
- Are two percent of total number of spaces or a minimum of one space set aside and designated for use by the physically disabled?
- Are special parking spaces clearly marked by signs?

Relative to walks and curbs:
- Are public walks at least 48 inches wide and have a gradient not greater than 5 percent?
- Is the gradient of walks and driveways less than that prescribed for ramps?
- Do walks of near maximum grade and considerable length have level areas at intervals for purposes of rest and safety?
- Do walks and driveways have nonslip surfaces?
- Do walks have a continuing common surface, not interrupted by steps or adrupt changes in level?
- Wherever walks cross other walks, driveways, or parking lots, do they blend to a common level?
- If a door swings out onto a platform or toward a walk, does the walk have a level platform at the top which is at least 5 feet by 5 feet?
- Does this platform extend at least 1 foot beyond each side of the doorway?
- If a door does not swing onto a platform or toward a walk, does the walk have a level platform at least 3 feet deep and 5 feet wide?
- Does this platform extend at least 1 foot beyond each side of the doorway?
- For walks with a slope greater than 5%, is there a handrail on one side?

Relative to ramps:
- Does a ramp have a slope greater than 1 foot rise in 12 feet, or 8.33 percent, or 4 degrees 50 minutes?

- Do ramps have handrails on at least one side, and preferably two sides, that are 32 inches in height?
- Where major traffic on ramps is predominately children, particularly physically disabled children, is extra care exercised in the placement of handrails in accordance with the nature of the facility and the age group or groups being served?
- Does the ramp have a surface that is nonslip?
- If a door swings out onto or toward the ramp, does the ramp have a level platform at the top which is at least 5 feet by 5 feet?
- If a door does not swing onto or toward the ramp, does the ramp have a level platform at least 3 feet deep and 5 feet wide?
- Does each ramp have at least 6 feet of straight clearance at the bottom?
- Do ramps have level platforms at 30-foot intervals for purposes of rest and safety?
- Do ramps have level platforms wherever they turn?
- Are curbs higher than the maximum height of one step—6½ inches?
- Do "double" or "stepped" curbs create unnecessary barriers to physically handicapped individuals?

Relative to stairs and rails:

- Do steps in stairs that might require use by those with disabilities or by the aged have abrupt (square) nosing?
- Do stairs have handrails 32 inches high as measured from the tread at the face of the riser?
- Where traffic on stairs is predominantly handicapped children, is extra care exercised in the placement of handrails in accordance with the nature of the facility and the age group or groups being served?
- Are dual handrails necessary for children and adults?
- Do stairs have at least one handrail that extends at least 18 inches beyond the top step and beyond the bottom step?
- Do steps have risers that exceed 7 inches?
- Is the minimum clear width for any stairway 3'-0"?
- Where stairs are heavily used, are stairway widths greater than 3'-0"?
- Is the maximum rise between landings for external unprotected stairs 4'-0"?
- Where the stairs are protected, is the maximum rise between landings 6'-0"?
- Do all stairway steps in a series have uniform tread width and riser height?
- Are stair treads deep enough to allow a man to place his whole foot on it?
- Is the stair tread death range between 11" to 14½"?
- Are risers for exterior stairs between 4" to 6½" in height?
- Are stairway nosings rounded or chamfered?
- Do stairways have an average maintained light level which ensures their safe use in darkness?
- Is light cast down toward risers so that the treads will not be in shadow?

- Are handrails and railings round or oval, 1½'' to 2'' in diameter?
- Is there a minimum 3'' spacing between handrails and adjacent walls?
- Is the wall surface nonabrasive?
- Where handrails or railing are fully recessed into walls, is there a space of 6'' between the top of the rail and the top of the recess, and a space of 3'' between the bottom of the rail and the bottom of the recess?
- Are the ends of handrails rounded off or turned into the wall so that they are not hazardous?
- Are handrails, railings and their appurtenances maintained free of slivers and sharp protrusions?
- Are handrails provided on both sides of every ramp?
- Do handrails on ramps extend past the heel and toe, 1'-0'' to 1'-6''?
- Is the vertical dimension from the ramp surface to the top of a single handrail between 2'-8'' and 3'-0''?
- Where two handrails are used on ramps, is the top rail placed at 3'-0'' to 3'-3'', and the lower rail placed at 2'-4''?
- Are handrails designed to support 250 lbs.?
- Are handrails securely fastened at all times on ramps or stairways?
- Are there raised numerals which indicate floor level and are fastened on the top of handrail extension near the end?

Relative to entrances and doors:
- Is there at least one primary entrance to each building usable by individuals in wheelchairs?
- Is there at least one entrance usable by individuals in wheelchairs on a level that would make elevators accessible?
- Do doors have a clear opening of no less than 32 inches when open and be operated by a single effort?
- Are two-leaf doors usable by non-ambulatory, semi-ambulatory, and coordination disabled individuals?
- Is the floor on the inside and outside of each doorway level for a distance of 5 feet from the door in the direction the door swings, and does the floor extend 1 foot beyond each side of the door?
- Are thresholds flush with the floor?
- Are door closers set in such a manner that they do not prevent the use of doors by the physically handicapped?
- Are time-delay door closers used?
- Are automatic doors used?
- Furniture and equipment should not have protrusions. Protruding elements create an obvious safety hazard to the user. The legs of a chair, for example, should not protrude past the outermost vertical plane of the chair;
- Furniture and equipment should not have edges which are sharp and composed of a dense material. Ideally, edges should be rounded and composed of or covered with a resilient material;
- The exterior of the human body lacks angularity and hardness. Furniture

and equipment should be curvilinear and resilient wherever possible in order to maximize comfort and minimize injury;

- Furniture and equipment should be viewed as objects which potentially give support to people. Furniture and equipment should, therefore, be stable and offer support to the user or the occasional passerby. Although the arms of a chair are used primarily for support, the back of a chair may also be considered as a possible support object. The back could be of a height, strength, and shape as to encourage its use as a railing;

- The disabled individual, in many cases, has greater difficulty interpreting the physical environment due to a physical, emotional, or visual disability. For this reason, elements within an object (the arms, legs, back and seat of a chair), between objects (a table and a chair), or between an object and its background (a drinking fountain and the wall it's mounted on) should be easily distinguished. In this manner, we can help to avoid confusion, injury to the individual, and damage to objects in the environment. Environmental clarity can be achieved by a variety of techniques, one of which is creating contrast with the use of color and/or texture. Another technique would be to allow space to occur between important elements of an object, i.e., that part of railing which is to be grasped. Objects intended to give support to the individual should especially be easily perceived. As an example, arms of a chair should be easily distinguishable from other elements of that chair, and easily identified from the background surfaces of the wall or floor;

- All children and adults require a sense of security and comfort in relation to their environment. However, the disabled individual has even a greater need. Physical solutions can greatly affect this relationship. The design of furniture and equipment may frustrate the child in the perception of his environment, or develop a sense of confidence toward the same environment. Furniture and equipment can work to give the feeling of safety and security, both physically and psychologically. For this reason, the following criteria should be used in the selection of furnishings and equipment: (a) objects and materials should not appear to be something other than what they are, (b) high reflecting finishes should be avoided to decrease confusing reflection and give clarity to the environment, (c) where large areas of glass are necessary, they should be carefully designed, (d) the design of furniture and equipment should maintain structural integrity, (e) the unnecessary use of mirrors and mirrored walls should be avoided, and (f) repetition of furniture and equipment layouts should be avoided where it will contribute to the confusion of the building user;

Relative to elevators: Unless ramps meeting the above requirements are provided to serve each floor level, is at least one elevator used that provided,

- All buildings over two stories in height with occupancy of 100 or more persons above or below the main entrance floor?
- All administrative buildings over one story?
- All publicly-owned school buildings and facilities over one story?
- All elevators accessible to, and usable by, the physically disabled at all levels normally used by the general public?
- Is the interior cab dimensions of elevators normally used by the public for buildings over three stories in height equal to or greater than 5 feet ×

5 feet square or 63 inches by 56 inches rectangular (a standard industrial size elevator)?
- In buildings three stories and less in height, is the elevator equal to or greater than 72″ × 44″ with a 2000 lb. capacity?
- Is the bottom of control panels no higher than four feet from the floor?
- Does the control panel use tacticle identification beside the buttons?

Relative to floors and corridors:
- Are corridors a minimum of five feet across?
- Are extended "seamless" surfaces of tile, carpeting or marble used, especially in hazardous transition locations (e.g., sidewalk-to-street)?
- Are all floors non-slip?
- Do the floors of a given story have a common level throughout?

Relative to classroom furniture and materials by type of handicap, the Educational Research Service's document *Barrier-Free School Facilities for Handicapped Students* includes an extensive description of appropriate furniture and materials for the (a) physically handicapped, (b) deaf and hard of hearing, (c) visually handicapped, (d) educably mentally retarded, (e) speech impaired, (f) emotionally disturbed, and (g) learning disabled. While no single standard can be applied to any specific handicapping condition, Berensons's comment concerning the learning disabled is applicable to all handicapping conditions:

> There remain many unanswered questions, simply because of the limited empirical evidence to support a specific architectural orientation toward the total relationship of behavior to environment. For this reason basic consideration . . . depend to a great extent on the designer's insights and his ability to interpret the operational intent of a given program.[9]

Regardless of type of handicapping condition, Abend makes the following suggestions concerning general criteria for selecting school furniture and equipment for the handicapped:
- The time and energy to use furnishings and equipment should be minimized;
- Setting should: (a) give support to the spinal lumbar curve, (b) avoid extremely hard seats which cause excessive compression of the flesh, (c) avoid excessive padding which increases pressure around the peripheral edges of the body and increases the difficulty of sitting down and rising, and (d) have seats which afford sufficient friction to avoid slipping;
- Furniture and equipment should be resistant to staining, scratching, chipping, and heat; and
- Furniture and equipment should be composed of nonallergenic materials.[10]

Relative to play spaces:
- Are there specifically environmentally controlled opportunities for gross and fine motor activities?

- Are there specifically environmentally controlled opportunities for encounters with elements and media that are distinctive to the outdoors?
- Are there specifically environmentally controlled opportunities for handicapped students to "perceive" spatial/temporal relationships such as height, width, before, after, etc.;
- Is all play space equipment readily accessible to handicapped children; and
- Is there *always* appropriate supervision of *all* play space equipment and activities?

Relative to sanitary facilities: there are several sources of information for designing barrier-free sanitary facilities. Minimum requirements include,

- Is there at least one toilet, for each sex on each floor, accessible to the physically handicapped?
- Are toilets located most distant from the facility's entrance?
- Is the stall door to the toilet have a 2 feet 8 inch opening clearance?
- Does the stall door swing out and not in?
- Is the stall at least 3 feet wide, and 4 feet 10 inches to 5 feet 6 inches deep?
- Is the toilet wall-mounted?
- Is the toilet seat 19 inches above the floor?
- Are grab bars, 1½ inches in diameter and 1½ inches from the walls, placed on both walls, 33 inches above the floor?
- Is there at least 26 inches of clear space between the floor and a sink?
- Are all faucet handles easy to operate?
- Are all hot water lines and drains under sinks shielded to protect the legs of handicapped children?
- Are all mirrors placed so that the bottom edge is not more than three feet above the floor level?
- Are all shower rooms with two or more stalls readily accessible to the handicapped?
- Do stalls measure 3 feet × 3 feet?
- Are shower room floor curbs no more than 2 inches above floor level?
- Is there a seat, positioned 19 inches above the floor, in each shower stall?
- Are shower stall seats hinged to fold against the wall?
- Is there a grab rail attached to the stall wall opposite the seat?
- Is the water control, diversionary shower spray, and soap tray placed 3 feet, 6 inches above the floor?
- Is there an appropriate number of toilet rooms, in accordance with the nature and use of a specific building or facility, accessible to, and usable by, the physically handicapped?
- Do toilet rooms have adequate spaces to allow traffic of handicapped individuals in wheelchairs?
- Do wall-mounted water closet's have narrow understructures that recede sharply?
- Do the wall-mounted water closet's have a front that is wide and

perpendicular to the floor at the front of the seat?
- Is the bowl of a wall-mounted water-closet shallow at the front of the seat and turned backward more than doward to allow handicapped individuals in wheelchairs to get close to the water closet with the seat of the wheelchair?
- Do toilet rooms for men have wall-mounted urinals with the opening of the basin 19 inches from the floor?
- Do toilet rooms have an appropriate number of towel racks, towel dispensers, and other dispensers and disposal units mounted no higher than 40 inches from the floor?

Relative to other facilities:
- Do all assembly places (e.g., theatres, auditoriums, courts, stadia, and arenas) with more than 75 seats reserve two percent, or at least two seats, of the total seating capacity for handicapped individuals in wheelchairs and/or with crutches and/or walkers?
- Are these reserved seats integrated with the general seating plan?
- Are such seats designed to conform with the requirements of accessibility for wheelchairs and crutches?
- Is there at least one student laboratory station provided to accommodate the physically handicapped?
- Does the laboratory station have a 30 inch clearance between the bottom of the work surface or apron and the floor?
- Is the laboratory station at least 18 inches deep and 30 inches wide?
- Are all hot water pipes insulated?
- Are faucets and utility outlets at laboratory stations side-mounted rather than rear-mounted and are they equipped with wrist blade or lever handles?
- Is the aisle leading to the laboratory space at least 36 inches wide?
- Is at least one percent of the study carrels and library tables accessible to the handicapped?
- Is there appropriate library assistance available to help handicapped individuals secure library materials?
- Are bookshelves not higher than 8 feet or lower than 9 inches above floor level?
- Is the aisle space between library stacks a minimum of 48 inches?
- Are card catalogues, dictionary stands, and other reference volumes 30 inches from the floor?
- Is there provision for soundproofing booths or study carrels where both blind and hard-of-hearing may use tape recorders, carousel projectors, and other audiovisual equipment?

Relative to controls and warning signals:
- Is there raised letters or numbers used to identify rooms or offices?
- Is such identification placed on the wall at a height between 4 feet 6 inches and 5 feet 6 inches?
- Are doors not intended for normal use, and that might prove dangerous

if a blind person were to exist or enter by them, quickly identifiable to the touch?
- Are facilities equipped with both audible and simultaneous visual warnings signals?

Relative to telephones:

- Is there at least one telephone accessible to the physically handicapped?
- Are all operating mechanisms (e.g., dial, headset, or coin slot) no more than 4 feet above the floor?
- Does the telephone have a headset?
- Does the headset have adjustable volume control with instructions?
- Is there visual and/or tactile instructions for using the telephone?
- Do telephone booths have at least 42 inches clear floor space between walls?
- Do telephone booths have at least 32 inches clear door openings with outswinging, sliding, or folding doors?
- Do telephone booths have a phone unit mounted on the side wall?
- Does the telephone booth seat fold up and out of the way?

In summary, "two general statements of philosophy . . . provide key starting points when administrators and architects are considering barrier-free design of classroom space and equipment.

- Generally, the more flexibility a teacher or teaching team has to restructure a learning environment rapidly and easily to meet specific needs and purposes, the better; and
- In general, design criteria for furniture and equipment in relation to disabled individuals are equally applicable to the design of furniture and equipment for the average person. The only difference is the degree that one can deviate from criteria . . . when considering the disabled person . . . compromise is inadvisable. While the average individual can easily adapt to undesirable conditions in the environment, the disabled person has a greater dependency upon the adherence to careful design."[11]

In determining the current program accessibility status based on a description of facilities, there are four fundamental questions that need to be addressed by the self-evaluation coordinator:

- Are the local educational agency's building code and facility construction specification readily available to the analyst?
- How concise and inclusive are these specifications?
- How accurate are current building code and construction specifications in comparison with actual building site construction?
- Can these building codes and construction specifications be used in lieu of examining each educational and non-educational facility in the district?

In developing the architectural barriers discrepancy analysis instrument, there are five fundamental questions that need to be addressed by the self-evaluation coordinator:

- How will the architectural barriers discrepancy analysis data gathering techniques to be used influence a discrepancy analysis instrument?
- What financial, personnel, or logistical problems are involved in developing the architectural barriers discrepancy analysis instrument?
- How reliable, valid, sensitive, appropriate, and objective is the architectural barriers discrepancy analysis instrument?
- What previous architectural barriers discrepancy analyses have been conducted and what techniques and instruments were employed?
- If there is no relevant previous use of the architectural barriers discrepancy analysis instrument, then has the analyst or self-evaluation coordinator conducted sufficient pilot studies to that the combination of the pilot data and his and others experience forms a sensible foundation for the content of the instrument?

In addition to the above five questions, the architectural barriers discrepancy analysis instrument should include:

- A directory of definitions for *all* pertinent discrepancy analysis variables; and
- A list of the district's specific program standard (e.g., the ANSI Standard).

Appendix A includes the checklist used in the Comptroller General's report to the Congress *Further Action Needed to Make all Public Buildings Accessible to the Physically Handicapped,"* [12] published July 15, 1975.

In determining data analysis methods, there are four fundamental questions that need to be addressed by the self-evaluation coordinator:

- What descriptive or inferential statistical techniques need to be used for the architectural barriers discrepancy analysis?
- While the statistical tests and discrepancy analysis design provide detailed and accurate information for administrative decision-making and program accessibility planning?
- Are the statistical tests and discrepancy analysis design such that school personnel can understand and use them without extensive training?

Conducting and analyzing components of the architectural barriers discrepancy analysis involves five decision-steps. These are:

- Delineating program accessibility discrepancy;
- Categorizing program accessibility discrepancies;
- Rank ordering program accessibility discrepancies;
- Delineating essential program accessibility discrepancies; and
- Preparing an architectural barriers discrepancy analysis profile including (a) recommendations for modifying the work environment, and (b) recommendations for modifying program accessibility for participants.

An examination of each of these five conducting and analyzing components follows.

From reviewing the local educational agency's building code, reviewing individual facility construction specifications, questioning/interviewing school personnel, and observing a select number of school facilities, the discrepancy analyst or self-evaluation coordinator is ready to delineate the status of each of the district's educational and non-educational facilities in relation to appropriate program accessibility standards. It is important that data be collected on *all* of the district's facilities, not just those facilities used for educational purposes. Qualified handicapped workers may be employed at maintenance facilities (e.g., bus garage) or administrative office facilities.

The simplest and most effective method of delineating program accessibility discrepancies is for the discrepancy analyst or self-evaluation coordinator to: (a) delineate for each educational and non-educational facility whether or not the facility meets all the requirements of the district's program accessibility standard (each specific standard can be written as a question which requires a "yes", "no", or "not applicable" response), and (b) describe (for each facility) the current architectural status of those facilities that do not meet specific standards. Therefore, an architectural barriers discrepancy analysis profile, in the form of a checklist, for each facility is necessary, as well as an discrepancy analysis profile that presents cumulative data for all facilities.

Once an architectural barrier discrepancy analysis profile has been obtained for each educational and non-educational facility, the discrepancy analyst should: (a) catergorize discrepancies in accordance with general program accessibility variables (e.g., access to classrooms, classroom facilities and materials, play spaces, sanitary facilities, other facilities, controls and warning signals, and telephones), and (b) rank ordering each facility by adding the total number of discrepancies, and rank ordering the cumulative scores for each specific standard for all facilities. The former information indicates which program variable categories will need to be examined for later program accessibility decision-making. The latter information indicates which facilities will need the most modifications made, and which specific program standard will need to be most frequently examined for all facilities.

Phase Vb: Modifying current procedures and practices

Phase Vb concerns the (a) modification of physical barriers impeding qualified handicapped workers from being employed or successfully fulfilling job responsibilities once employed, and (b) modification of physical barriers impeding handicapped individuals from successfully participating in a district's programs and activities. At this point, the self-evaluation coordinator can make specific recommendations concerning: (a) architectural barriers program accessibility modifications needed to provide qualified handicapped individuals with appropriate employment and program accessibility opportunities, and (b) the degree of compliance between a local educational agency's program accessibility provisions and Section 504, Subpart C regulation. Also, as indicated when modifying employment practices and procedures, the role and responsibilities of the self-evaluation coordinator can be either: (a) terminated while administrative decision-makers debate and/or implement the self-evaluator's recommendations and suggestions, or (b) altered in accordance with Scriven's goal free evaluation approach so that the self-evaluation coordinator begins assisting in the developmental planning and implementing of alternate program accessibility practices and procedures.

As when addressing the problems of costs, benefits, and economic impact of implementing alternate staffing practices and procedures, the author has included O'Neill's (paraphrased and slightly modified) report *Discrimination Against Handicapped Persons: The Costs, Benefits, and Economic Impact of Implementing Section 504 of the Rehabilitation Act of 1973 Concerning Recipients of HEW Financial Assistance.*[13]

> As stated previously, Section 504, Subpart C regulation prohibits the exclusion of qualified handicapped persons by reason of the inaccessibility of a recipients facilities. Subpart C applies to all programs and recipients covered by the Section 504 regulation. Two standards are established for program accessibility—one for new construction (Paragraph 84.23), the other for existing buildings (Paragraph 84.22).
>
> Under Paragraph 84.23, new construction and design must, at a minimum, either meet the standards for barrier-free construction established by the American National Standards Institute or provide equivalent access. Any alternation or portions of existing buildings which is undertaken must also provide ready access if the alternation involves work on a portion of the facility which could affect usability (e.g., toilets, elevators, stairs, and curbs). All Federal and Federally assisted construction is subject to virtually identical requirements under the Architectural Barriers Act, P.L. 90-480.
>
> Under Paragraph 84.22 (covering existing facilities) each program or activity, when viewed in its entirety, must, within three years of the effective date of the regulation, be physically accessible to handicapped persons. Because of the flexibility allowed by the regulation, it is expected that most recipients will be able to achieve compliance without incurring excessive costs. However, the Department of Health, Education and Welfare recognizes that in certain cases the cost of compliance can be excessive, and that in rare cases, compliance through renovation will be impossible for structural and/or cost reasons.
>
> The following presents a range of estimates of the aggregate cost of compliance for both new and existing facilities. Although the estimates lack precision, they do give some idea of the magnitude of the costs which will be incurred. After the cost estimates, the sources of benefits are indicated and alternatives are considered.
>
> For new construction, the Office of Facilities, Engineering and Property Management (OFEPM), Department of Health, Education and Welfare, recommends that for budget purposes the cost of barrier-free construction should be estimated at one-half of one percent of the total project cost. Other estimates are considerably below this, with some as little as one-tenth of one percent.
>
> This low percentage increase, coupled with the fact that compliance is to be achieved over the years as new structures are erected, renders the economic impact of the provision minimal. For example, the National Center for Education Statistics estimates that gross outlays for new plant by institutions of higher education was $3.4 billion during the 1975-76 school year. If we assume that $2.0 billion represented new additions and use .003 as our percentage cost factor, then an extra capital outlay of $6

million per year is indicated. This is equivalent to an "annual cost" of about $.6 million per year. Total current operating expenditures in 1975-76 were about $38 billion, which means the addition to the annual cost of providing higher education of having all new buildings barrier-free is only about 2 thousandths of one percent. The existence of substantially duplicative state and Federal requirements reduces the impact even further. This does not mean that the importance of the enforcement of the regulation for new construction is unimportant. The additional cost is negligible only as long as the building has not yet been erected. However, the cost of correcting a noncompliance after the building is up is much greater since the costs of modifications rise sharply.

Since the first publication of proposed regulation (*Federal Register*, May 17, 1976, Part V), concern has been expressed by a number of recipients about the cost of bringing their existing facilities into compliance. Most of the apprehension expressed revolved around two issues—the meaning and content of the phrase "program accessibility" and whether or not the regulation would be enforced in impossible situations or where the cost of modification would be clearly excessive. More specifically, what is meant by the concept of "program accessibility" as opposed to "barrier-free environment"? and what is implied by the phrase, "A recipient shall, through the elimination of physical obstacles or through other methods, operate each program or activity to which this . . . applies so that the program or activity, when viewed in its entirety, is readily accessible to handicapped persons?" In general, both issues can be answered by stating that Section 504 regulation does not require that each facility or every part of a facility must be accessible, let alone barrier-free. However, Section 504 regulation does require that when a handicapped applicant appears and the recipient is confronted with an impossible situation or one that involves clearly excessive cost to change a building's physical features, he may achieve compliance by providing a reasonable substitute for actual physical access on the part of the handicapped individual.

Some examples of these situations and possible allowable substitutions are:

- The stacks in the libraries of some schools, especially older schools, have very narrow halls and aisles and are located on upper floors of buildings built many years ago so that elevator access is either nonexistent or is of such tiny dimensions as to make access via a wheelchair impossible without extensive modification. In this case, a reasonable substitute for direct physical access would be the assignment of personnel to supply occasional individualized "stack search" for handicapped students on request;
- In cases in which a curriculum can be offered only in a particular facility which would be exceedingly expensive or impossible to modify or relocate and in which only rarely would a mobile handicapped person be expected to apply, an institution would have the option of making that modification or paying the differential costs (primarily travel) of attending another institution with a comparable offering in accessible surroundings. Another strategy might involve the substitution of equivalent courses, especially in the case of elective courses;
- A situation that will probably be faced most frequently by older schools is gaining access to classrooms on the upper floors in buildings with no elevators. The most obvious substitute for making all classrooms in the

building physically accessible is to reschedule the class in question to an accessible classroom.

There will, of course, be rare situations in which a handicapped applicant appears and no substitute for providing expensive physical access is possible. For example, if the classroom on the upper floor in a non-elevator building happens to be the only chemistry lab for secondary school students. Another extreme case is when the school campus itself is located in a very inaccessible terrain. That the foregoing types of situations exist is certain, but how numerous they are among all school districts is not clear.

The question of whether or not to allow exceptions in impossible cases or in cases where the cost of compliance would clearly be excessive is very controversial. Opponents argue that allowing exceptions would lead to segregation of handicapped individuals as well as a reduced range of choice and opportunity. Also, there is concern that, in practice, exceptions will become a "loophole" through which local educational agencies confronted with only reasonable costs of complying with program accessibility will avoid compliance.

One argument advanced in favor of allowing exceptions in impossible situations or cases where the cost is clearly excessive is based on the relatively small number of handicapped students that would be likely to attend schools possessing features which would be either impossible to remove or excessively costly to remove. The argument is that without any exceptions there would be a sizeable amount of expenditure for remodeling that would be utilized by only a very small number of handicapped students. It appears that no more than 300,000 children ages 0 to 19 have the kind of handicaps that inhibit them from gaining access to the average building. Clearly, only the categories crippled and physically impaired, multihandicapped, and visually impaired contain individuals who have trouble gaining access to buildings, and the total children in these categories is only approximately 434,000. Thus, 300,000 is clearly biased upward because some fraction of the categories have impairments that do not hamper them in gaining access to buildings. In effect, the argument for making exceptions in these cases is that impossible situations can be resolved and major costs avoided by utilizing alternatives without decreasing benefits significantly. While the regulation does not provide for exceptions per se, language in the preamble of the proposed regulation suggests that, in accordance with its customary procedures, the Office for Civil Rights will not require the impossible. Thus, alternatives to renovation will be allowed in situations of impossibility or where the cost of compliance would be clearly excessive. The cost estimates of this statement assume that, even without explicit exceptions, enforcement will, in practice, allow reasonable alternatives in truly exceptional cases. As a consequence of this assumption, it is apparent that no major savings would result from the inclusion of provisions for specific exceptions in the corpus of the regulation.

Another possible standard for existing facilities is to allow "program accessibility" to be an interim, or short run standard but to require a "barrier-free'' standard be met in the long run—say 15 to 20 years. This, of course, adds to the overall cost of compliance whether or not exceptions are allowed for some types of situations. However, the amount of increase is minimized by allowing such a long time period for compliance. During this period of time many buildings will have been erected and these costs have already been accounted for under new facilities. Also, the present outlays required to cover costs far in the future tend to be much less because, in principle, funds can be set aside to earn a positive rate of interest.

Our estimate of the total cost of altering enough existing facilities and making all the required substitute adjustments for all categories of recipients (universities and colleges, elementary and secondary schools, hospitals, welfare offices) to meet the standard of program accessibility is between $299 and $544 million, or an annualized cost of between $30 and $55 million.

Our range of estimate is $182 million to $283 million for all elementary and secondary school systems to achieve compliance. These estimates were derived by multiplying an estimate of the value of all elementary and secondary school buildings at the end of school year 1973-1974, $101.0 billion, by aggregate cost factors of .0018 and .0028. They are derived from the cost factor used for higher education—.0056. Recall that this factor assumed that all affected campuses would make all of their buildings accessible (but not necessarily all the floors in any building). Recall also that his factor assumes that exceptions may be made in impossible cases and cases of excessive cost. However, for elementary and secondary schools, it seems plausible to assume that the average system will have to make, at most, ½ and may even be able to achieve compliance with as few as ⅓. Thus, .0018 = .3 × .0056 and .0028 = .5 × .0056.

We noted above that only a small fraction of all handicapped children have those kinds of impairments that hamper their gaining access to the average school building. And since only 10% of all school children have any kind of handicap at all, only a very small fraction of all school children are involved. Thus, most school systems should be able (by providing the required transportation to assign all of their physically handicapped children to a few of their buildings. For example, even a moderate size school system (say with only 10-15 separate buildings) with no new or already accessible buildings, should have to modify only one or two of its buildings.

There are many factors which might affect the percentage of buildings which need to be accessible if the local eudcational agency is to comply with Section 504 regulation. We shall mention several of these and explain briefly how these factors may affect the cost of compliance.

- The number of buildings currently accessible will influence the cost by decreasing the amount of renovation necessary;
- The number of buildings present will influence the cost since the greater the number of buildings, the larger the number of scheduling options and the less likelihood that very unsuitable buildings will need to be renovated;
- The size of the buildings will influence the cost since greater individual

size tends to increase scheduling options in a single unit, thereby, potentially reducing the number of units that need renovation;

- The enrollment of the institution can influence the cost since a wider range of course/section scheduling options is frequently concomitant with greater size. However, smaller enrollment may sometimes imply greater flexibility because of simplified scheduling demands and decreased demands of space;
- Faculty-student ratios may influence cost of compliance since smaller classes are often easier to reschedule and relocate;
- The overall content of a program will influence the cost in several ways. The number of majors offered may increase scheduling problems and, hence, increase the number of buildings needing renovation. Curricula in which relatively little specialized equipment is used may influence cost of compliance by reducing the need to incur costs of making laboratories, etc. accessible. The presence of a highly structured core curriculum may raise the cost since such programs frequently have rigid scheduling requirements.

The fact that there are many influential, variables affecting cost points to the necessity of evaluating each educational and non-educational facility individually.

Increased building accessibility will generate benefits in three areas: (a) reduced costs of providing elementary and secondary education to some handicapped children, (b) increased lifetime earnings capacity of those additional handicapped youngsters who will not go on to college, and (c) the increased earnings capacity of handicapped workers who can now find better employment in their skills in jobs located in newly accessible buildings.

Each of these areas is also the subject of its own subpart—elementary and secondary education (Subpart D), higher education, (Subpart E) and employment (Subpart B). The total amount of benefits for each of these areas will be the sum of the benefits produced by both the physical accessibility provisions of this subpart and the other (non-accessibility) provisions of each specific subpart. Thus, in Subpart B, we estimated that the total amount of pecuniary benefits from all the provisions influencing employment discrimination (i.e., procedural provisions, non-accessibility accommodations and accessibility accommodations) might be as much as $1 billion per year. Similarly, in our analyses of Subparts D and E, we can include the effects of both the accessibility provisions of this subpart and the other non-accessibility provisions of each of those subparts.

Possible alternatives for program accessibility range from requiring the immediate modification of all of the school district's existing facilities to limiting the regulation's coverage to only the most inaccessible facilities, particularly existing facilities. The approach finally decided upon, which allows school district to keep costs minimal by using methods other than physical alteration of all buildings, is believed to constitute the most equitable balance between the interests of excluded handicapped individuals and those of local educational agencies. The cost estimates shown above, when combined with evidence presented elsewhere on the magnitude of the benefits that will be generated, lends support to this decision.

As in the case of employment practices discussed in Chapter II, there is a potential difficulty created by the regulation's use of the term "reasonable" rather than some more specific threshold (e.g., "not to exceed a certain sum of money per client benefited"). However, no satisfactory solution to the wording of such an approach has been devised, and such an approach could be as or more difficult to interpret in practice as the approach chosen.

Chapter IV

P.L. 94-142 and Section 504: Comparison and Contrast

Subpart D of Section 504 regulation requires that recipients of Department of Health, Education and Welfare financial assistance that operate public elementary and secondary education programs must provide a free appropriate public education to each qualified handicapped individual who is in the recipient's jurisdiction, regardless of the nature or severity of the individual's handicap. Public Law 94-142, The Education For All Handicapped Children Act, requires that recipient's of Part B financial assistance of the Education of the Handicapped Act (P.L. 91-230) must (a) assure that all handicapped children have available to them a free appropriate public education, and (b) assure that the rights of handicapped children and their parents are protected. The Department of Health, Education and Welfare, which has authority over both Section 504 regulation and P.L. 94-142, developed Subpart D provisions in "close coordination" with the regulation for P.L. 94-142. In general, Section 504, Subpart D regulation and P.L. 94-142 statute and regulation requires that HEW recipient's of financial aid operating public education programs provide a free appropriate education to each qualified handicapped child in the most normal setting appropriate.

Section 504, Subpart D regulation generally conforms to the standards established for the education of handicapped individuals in Mills v. Board of Education of the District of Columbia (1972), Pennsylvania Association for Retarded Children v. Commonwealth of Pennsylvania (1971), and LeBanks v. Spears (1973, as well as in the Education of the Handicapped Act (P.L. 91-230), as amended by Public Law 94-142, The Education for All Handicapped Children Act.

The basic requirements common to the court cases and legislative statutes and administrative agency regulation are:
- That handicapped individual's, regardless of the nature or severity of their handicap, be provided a free appropriate public education;
- That handicapped students be educated with nonhandicapped students to the maximum extent appropriate to their needs;

- That educational agencies undertake to identify and locate all unserved handicapped children;
- That evaluation procedures be improved in order to avoid the inappropriate education that results from the misclassification of students; and
- That procedural safeguards be established to enable parents and guardians to influence decisions regarding the evaluation and placement of their children.

These requirements are designed to ensure that no handicapped child is excluded from school on the basis of handicap and, if a recipient educational setting cannot be achieved satisfactorily, that the student is provided with adequate alternative services suited to the student's needs without additional cost to the student's parents or guardian.

The remaining portion of Chapter IV examines Section 504, Subpart D regulation in relation to applicable P.L. 94-142 statute and regulation. It is not the intention of the author to provide an all-inclusive or exhaustive examination of the various comparable and contrasting provisions of Section 504, Subpart D and P.L. 94-142. Such an undertaking is beyond the scope of this handbook. For those interested in an extensive examination of Section 504 regulation and P.L. 94-142 statute and regulation, the author recommends the National Association of State Directors of Special Education's documents *The Rehabilitation Act: An Analysis of the Section 504 Regulation and Its Implications for State and Local Education Agencies,*[1] and *Section 504/P.L. 94-142: A Comparison of Selected Provisions of the Proposed Regulations for Section 504 of The Vocational Rehabilitation Act of 1973 and Selected Provisions of P.L. 94-142, The Education For All Handicapped Children Act of 1975.*[2]

General provisions

In Subpart A, Paragraph 84.1, the purpose of the Section 504 regulation is enumerated.

The purpose of this part is to effectuate Section 504 of the Rehabilitation Act of 1973, which is designed to eliminate discrimination on the basis of handicap in any program or activity receiving Federal financial assistance.

The application of Section 504 regulation is stated in Paragraph 84.2.

This part applies to each recipient of Federal financial assistance from the Department of Health, Education and Welfare and to each program or activity that receives or benefits from such assistance.

In general, Section 504 regulation is an extension of the civil rights provisions of Title VI of the Civil Rights Act of 1964 and Title IX of The Education Amendments of 1972 (applying, respectively, to racial discrimination and to discrimination in education on the basis of sex). Therefore, Section 504 regulation should be included under the rubric "civil rights act" (even though Section 504 is nearly all regulation, not statute). *Without exception,* Section 504 regulation is applicable to *all* 50 states, and, consequently, to all local, intermediate, and State educational agencies.

In contrast, Public Law 94-142 applies only to those states which receive financial assistance under Part B of The Education of the Handicapped Act (P.L. 91-230). P.L. 94-142 statute and regulation govern the provision of formula grant funds to State and local educational agencies to assist them in the education of handicapped children. P.L. 94-142 is *not* a "civil rights act". If a state does not accept Part B funds of The Education of the Handicapped Act (P.L. 91-230), the state is not required to comply with P.L. 94-142 regulation. One very important point needs to be emphasized: all states and their local educational agencies, regardless whether or not they submit for Part B funds, *must* comply with Section 504 regulation. Therefore, refusal to submit for Part B funds of The Education of the Handicapped Act does not abrogate any school district from providing the basic civil rights provisions of Section 504 regulation.

Being a "civil rights act", Section 504 regulation encompasses a broad range of topics: (a) employment practices, (b) program accessibility, (c) preschool, elementary, and secondary education, (d) post secondary education, (e) health, welfare, and social services, and (f) complaint and enforcement procedures. Being a formula grant act, P.L. 94-142 is concerned with providing financial assistance to assist states and localities to provide for the education of all handicapped children and to assess and ensure the effectiveness of efforts to educate those children. In general, Section 504, Subpart D regulation delineates the broad civil rights provisions necessary for all State and local educational agencies, while P.L. 94-142, in its entirety, delineates the specific substantive and procedural requirements to effectively implement the intent of Section 504, Subpart D provisions. This contrast of general and specific requirements is noted by the Department of Health, Education and Welfare.

> The very complex general language of Section 504 and the scant legislative history surrounding its enactment provide little guidance as to how complex issues should be resolved.

While,

> Because the statute P.L. 94-142 is very comprehensive and specific on many points . . . the Department sees the development of regulation for implementing P.L. 94-142 as being an evolutionary process which will continue over a period of several years.

Enforcement of Section 504 regulation is the responsibility of The Office for Civil Rights, Department of Health, Education and Welfare. Enforcement of P.L. 94-142 statute and regulation is the responsibility of the Bureau of Education for the Handicapped, Department of Health, Education and Welfare.

For the implementation of Section 504 requirements, the responsibility is for the individual states and the local educational agencies to provide sufficient funds. Section 504 regulation does *not* provide for any Federal financial assistance to implement its civil rights provisions. For the implementation of P.L. 94-142, the responsibility is jointly shared by the Federal government (who will provide funds to assist in financing the excess cost of educating handicapped students) and local educational agencies (who must provide for an "average minimum amount" for the education of handicapped students). Therefore, both Section 504 regulation and P.L. 94-142 place the majority responsibility with State and local educational agencies for funding the education of the handicapped.

Probably the single most important point of contrast between Section 504 regulation and P.L. 94-142 statute and regulation concerns the definition of "handicapped person" in Section 504 and "handicapped children" in P.L. 94-142. A "handicapped person" is any person who: (a) has a physical or mental impairment which substantially limits one or more major life activities, (b) has a record of such an impairment, or (c) is regarded as having such an impairment. Incorporated in this definition are the more specific terms:

- Major life activities—functions such as caring for one's self, performing manual tasks, walking, seeing, hearing, speaking, breathing, learning, and working;
- Has a record of such an impairment—has a history of, or has been misclassified as having, a mental or physical impairment that substantially limits one or more major life activities; and
- Is regarded as having an impairment—means (a) having a physical or mental impairment that does not substantially limit major life activities but that is treated by a recipient as constituting such a limitation, (b) has a physical or mental impairment that substantially limits major life activities only as a result of the attitudes of others toward such impairment, or (c) has none of these impairments but is treated by a recipient as having such an impairment.

Included in this definition of "handicapped person" are physiological disorders or conditions and any mental or psychological disorders. Also included in this definition are not only educationally recognized "handicapping" conditions (e.g., neurological damage, mental retardation, or specific learning disabilities), but also drug addiction and alcoholism.

A "handicapped child" is any child who has been evaluated as being mentally retarded, hard of hearing, deaf, speech impaired, visually handicapped, seriously emotionally disturbed, orthopedically impaired, other health impaired, deaf-blind, multihandicapped, or as having specific learning disabilities, who because of these impairments, need special education and related services.

In general, the term "handicapped person" covers a very broad range of actual or perceived handicapping conditions, while the term "handicapped child" covers a more specific range of educational or medical conditions, appropriately identified and evaluated.

Location and notification

Paragraph 84.32 of Section 504, Subpart D requires that a recipient that operates a public elementary or secondary education program must annually:

- Undertake to identify and locate every qualified handicapped individual residing in the recipient's jurisdiction who is not receiving a public education; and
- Take appropriate steps to notify handicapped individuals and their

parents or guardian of the recipient's duty to provide a free appropriate public education.

Paragraph 121a.220 of P.L. 94-142 regulation requires that local educational agencies must include in their Part B applications procedures which ensure that all children residing within the jurisdiction of the local educational agency who are handicapped, regardless of the severity of their handicap, and who are in need of special education and related services are identified, located, and evaluated. Also, Paragraph 121a.226 of P.L. 94-142 regulation requires that local educational agencies must develop and employ procedures to ensure that provision is made for the participation of and consultation with parents or guardians of handicapped children.

Free appropriate public education

Paragraph 84.33 of Section 504, Subpart D regulation requires that a recipient that operates a public elementary or secondary education program must provide a free appropriate public education to each qualified handicapped individual who is in the recipient's jurisdiction, regardless of the nature or severity of the individual's handicap. The provision of an appropriate education is the provision of regular or special education and related aids and services that: (a) are designed to meet individual educational needs of handicapped persons as adequately as the needs of nonhandicapped individuals are met, and (b) are based upon adherence of procedures that satisfy the requirements of educational setting, evaluation and placement, and procedural safeguard.

Paragraph 121a.121 of P.L. 94-142 regulation requires that each State and local educational agency has in effect a policy which ensures that all handicapped children have the right to a free appropriate public education within the ranges of three through twenty-one by September 1, 1980. Paragraph 121a.4 defines free appropriate public education as special education and related services which:

- Are provided at public expense, under public supervision and direction, and without charge;
- Meet the standards of the State educational agency;
- Include preschool, elementary, and secondary education programs; and
- Are provided in conformity with an individualized education program which meets the unique needs of each handicapped child.

It is important to note that Section 504, Subpart D regulation recognizes that implementation of an individualized education program developed in accordance with the Education of the Handicapped Act (as amended by P.L. 94-142) is one means of obtaining the standard of meeting individual educational needs of handicapped students.

Paragraph 84.33 (b)(3) of Section 504, Subpart D regulation stipulates that a local educational agency may place a handicapped individual in or refer such an individual to a program other than the one that it operates as its means of carrying out the requirements of providing a free appropriate public education.

Subpart D of P.L. 94-142 regulation concerns the referring or placing of handicapped children in private schools by local educational agencies. Subpart D of P.L. 94-142 regulation requires that each State educational agency shall ensure that a handicapped child who is placed in or referred to a private school or facility by a local educational agency: (a) is provided special education and related services, and (b) has all of the rights of a handicapped child who is served by a public agency. Also, the State educational agency must monitor private school compliance through procedures such as written reports, on-site visits, and parent questionnaires. Paragraphs 84.33(c)(3) of Section 504 regulation and 121a.302 of P.L. 94-142 regulation stipulate that if placement in a public or private residential program is necessary, the program, including non-medical care and room and board, must be at no cost to the parents of the child.

Educational setting

Paragraph 84.34 of Section 504, Subpart D regulation stipulates that local educational agencies must educate each qualified handicapped individual in its jurisdiction with individuals who are not handicapped to the maximum extent appropriate to the needs of the handicapped individual. Also, a local educational agency must place a handicapped individual in the regular educational environment unless it is demonstrated by the school district that the education of the handicapped individual in the regular environment with the use of supplementary aids and services cannot be achieved satisfactorily. Paragraphs 121a.550 through 121a.556 of P.L. 94-142 regulation delineate the concept of least restrictive environment. Specifically, each local educational agency must ensure:

- That to the maximum extent appropriate, handicapped children, including children in public or private institutions or other care facilities, are educated with children who are not handicapped; and
- That special classes, separate schooling or other removal of handicapped children from the regular educational environment occures only when the nature or severity of the handicap is such that education in regular classes with the use of supplementary aids and services cannot be achieved satisfactorily.

Paragraphs 84.34(b) of Section 504 regulation and 121a.553 of P.L. 94-142 regulation require that in providing or arranging for the provision of nonacademic and extracurricular services and activities, each local educational agency must ensure that each handicapped child participates with nonhandicapped children in those services and activities to the maximum extent appropriate to the needs of that child.

Paragraphs 84.34(c) of Section 504, Subpart D regulation and 121a.231 of P.L. 94-142 regulation stipulates that facilities, services, and activities identified as being for handicapped individuals are comparable to other facilities, services, and activities of the school district.

Evaluation and placement

Paragraph 84.35 of Section 504 regulation requires that local educational

agencies conduct an evaluation of any child who, because of a handicap, needs or is believed to need special education or related services before taking any action with respect to the initial placement of the child in a particular or special education program and any subsequent significant change in placement. Standards and procedures for evaluation and placement should include:
- Tests and other evaluation materials have been validated for the specific purpose for which they are used and are administered by trained personnel in conformance with the instructions provided by their producer;
- Tests and other evaluation materials include those tailored to assess specific areas of educational need and not merely those which are designed to provide a single general intelligence quotient; and
- Tests are selected and administered so as best to ensure that, when a test is administered to a student with impaired sensory, manual, or speaking skills, the test results accurately reflect the student's aptitude or achievement level or whatever other factor the test purports to measure, rather than reflecting the student's impaired sensory, manual, or speaking skills (except where those skills are the factors that the test purports to measure).

P.L. 94-142 regulation (Paragraph 121a.532) includes the above evaluation requirements, and also includes:
- No single procedure is used as the sole criterion for determining an appropriate educational program for a child;
- The evaluation is made by a multidisciplinary team or group of persons, including at least one teacher or other specialist with knowledge in the area of suspected disability; and
- The child is assessed in all areas related to the suspected disability, including where appropriate, health, vision, hearing, social and emotional status, general intelligence, academic performance, communicative status, and motor abilities.

Paragraphs 84.35(c) of Section 504, Subpart D regulation and 121a.533 of P.L. 94-142 regulation require that in interpreting evaluation data and in making placement decisions, a school district must:
- Draw upon information from a variety of services, including aptitude and achievement tests, teacher recommendations, physical condition, social or cultural background, and adaptive behavior;
- Establish procedures to ensure that information obtained from all such sources is documented and carefully considered;
- Ensure that the placement decision is made by a group of persons, including persons knowledgeable about the child, the meaning of the evaluation data, and the placement options; and
- Ensure that the placement decisions is made in the least restrictive environment.

Procedural safeguards

Paragraph 84.36 of Section 504, Subpart D regulation requires that a local educational agency establish and implement with respect to actions regarding the identification, evaluation, or educational placement of individuals who, because of handicaps, need or are believed to need special instruction or related services, a system of procedural safeguards that includes notice, an opportunity for the parents or guardian of the individual to examine relevant records, an impartial hearing with opportunity for participation by the individual's parents/guardian and representation by counsel, and a review procedure. Subpart E of P.L. 94-142 regulation encompasses all of these requirements while providing for more specificity for each. The Department of Health, Education and Welfare notes that compliance with the procedural safeguards of Section 615 of the Education of the Handicapped Act (as amended by P.L. 94-142) is one means of meeting Section 504, Subpart D requirements.

Nonacademic services

Paragraphs 84.37 of Section 504, Subpart D regulation and 121a.306-307 of P.L. 94-142 regulation stipulate that a local educational agency must provide nonacademic and extracurricular services and activities in such manner as is necessary to afford handicapped students an equal opportunity for participation in such services and activities. Nonacademic and extracurricular services and activities may include counseling services, physical recreational athletics, transportation, health services, recreational activities, special interest groups or clubs sponsored by the district, referrals to agencies which provide assistance to handicapped individuals, and employment of students, including both employment by the district and assistance in making available outside employment.

A local educational agency that provides personal, academic, or vocational counseling, guidance, or placement services to its students must provide these services without discrimination on the basis of handicap. Furthermore, the school district shall ensure that qualified handicapped students are not counseled toward more restrictive career objectives than are nonhandicapped students with similar interests and abilities.

In providing physical education courses and athletics, the local educational agency must provide to qualified handicapped students an equal opportunity for participation in these activities. A school district may offer to handicapped students physical education and athletic activities that are separate or different from those offered to nonhandicapped students only if separation or differentiation is consistent with the least restrictive environment requirements and only if no qualified handicapped student is denied the opportunity to compete for teams or to participate in courses that are not separate or different.

Chapter V

Future Issues

Probably no other single statement characterizes both Section 504 of the Rehabilitation Act of 1973 and Public Law 94-142, The Education for All Handicapped Children Act, better than that made by Alan Abeson in 1976 and included in the Introduction to *Public Law 94-142: Special Education in Transition*. Examining the effects of the "quiet revolution" in establishing for the handicapped the same education rights afforded the non-handicapped, Abeson concluded that American social values had entered an "era in which the battle cry for public policy advance changed from charitable solicitations to a declaration of rights." In terms of public policy, Section 504 represents the first Federal civil rights law protecting the rights of handicapped individuals and reflects the national commitment to end discrimination on the basis of handicap. In terms of declaring rights, Section 504 not only establishes a mandate to end discrimination, but requires that handicapped individuals be brought into the mainstream of American society.

While the Office for Civil Rights of the Department of Health, Education and Welfare "intends vigorously to implement and enforce that mandate", DHEW also recognizes that the problem of ending discrimination on the basis of handicap presents considerations that are extremely complex. Elaborating this point in the May 4, 1977 final regulation for Section 504, Joseph Califano, Jr., Secretary, Department of Health, Education and Welfare, observed that "there is overwhelming evidence that in the past many handicapped persons have been excluded from programs. But eliminating such gross exclusions and denials of equal treatment is not sufficient to assure genuine equal opportunity. In drafting a regulation to prohibit exclusion and discrimination, it became clear that different or special treatment of handicapped persons, because of their handicaps may be necessary in a number of contexts in order to ensure equal opportunity."

The fundamental concept underlying Section 504 regulation is that of "reasonable accommodation" must be afforded the known physical or mental limitations of qualified handicapped program applicants or employees unless demonstrable evidence is provided that accommodation would impose an undue hardship on program operation. In defining reasonable accommodation, emphasis is placed on program accessibility and employment restructuring. While this emphasis may facilitate immediate relief to handicapped individuals in participating in Federally assisted program and activities, and in ensuring appropriate employment opportunities, the burden of responsibility rests with all private and public institutions and organizations to incorporate the basic principle of reasonable accommodation for the handicapped. However, several important issues need to be examined first, before handicapped individuals can be successfully brought into the mainstream of American society, and second, before public school administrators can appropriately plan, implement, and evaluate modifications in program structure and operation. Some of these issues are:

- American society in general, and the public school system in particular, has found that remediating previous discriminatory practices both complex and difficult, regardless of the minority population involved. Experience with Title VI of the Civil Rights Act of 1964 (concerning race discrimination) and Title IX of the Education Amendments of 1972 (concerning sex discrimination) has proven that, even when discrimination has been based on presumably innocuous human characteristics (e.g., race and sex), simply mandating that these characteristics be eliminated as determining factors in program structure and operation has proven to be only the initial step in affecting social change. With Section 504 regulation, the remediation required of all public and private institutions and organizations receiving Federal financial assistance moves from eliminating innocuous human characteristics as determining factors to considering reasonable accommodation for known or suspected physical or mental limitations. Such a major alteration will necessitate leadership being exerted at and by all levels of Federal, state, and local government and their instrumentalities (such as public school systems). Without sufficient guidance and the fiscal, human, and material resources to implement program modifications, it is presumptuous to assume that the intent of Section 504 will affect either individual or organizational behavior. Future issues in administrative decision-making should include: (a) clarifying what constitutes reasonable accommodation, (b) determining who defines reasonable accommodation and for what social, educational, or political purposes, and (c) determining how significant modifications in program structure and operation can be obtained without incurring unnecessary disruptions in service delivery;
- The Department of Health, Education and Welfare notes that "the very general language of Section 504 itself and the scant legislative history surrounding its enactment provide little guidance as to how these complex issues should be resolved." This lack of Federal guidance has two advantages: first, it can afford diversity and flexibility in administrative decision-making, and second, it allows for an evolutionary process for social change. However, there is one major disadvantage with this lack of Federal guidance. Many decision-makers, including public school administrators, fear judicial or legislative retribution based on post hoc determinations of legal compliance with Section 504

regulation. This fear may cause school administrators to rigidly adhere to specific legal requirements without taking the leadership position that is necessary for affecting "real" as opposed to "paper" changes in program operation and structure and societal values and attitudes. Future issues should include: (a) determining how public school administrators can effectively exert leadership in affecting social change without abrogating legal responsibilities, (b) determining how the greatly increased role of the Federal government in local regular and special education programming can benefit both handicapped and nonhandicapped individuals without unduly usurping the authority of local governments, organizations, and institutions, and (c) determining how the "least restrictive alternative doctrine" (see Chapter III in *Public Law 94-142: Special Education in Transition*) can balance fundamental individual interests with legitimate and compelling state interests (e.g., determining what constitutes reasonable accommodation in State public school systems);

- And finally, will the concept of reasonable accommodation have a positive or negative effect on individual and program performance effectiveness? Future issues should include: (a) does an organization or institution have the "right" to employ individuals, handicapped or not, that are not only qualified for a specific position, but in fact have more than minimal or essential skills or competencies as delineated in a job analysis study? (b) if so, how will this affect the employment of qualified handicapped applicants? and (c) if not, will the concept of meritorious organizational and individual behavior become constricted within a maze of legal regulations and restrictions?

In conclusion, Section 504 regulation, in concert with P.L. 94-142, can provide much needed relief to handicapped individuals in obtaining employment and educational opportunities, and in participating in Federally assisted programs and activities. However, many administrative decision-making issues need to be addressed before Section 504 requirements can be successfully achieved. In concluding, the author once again quotes David Mathews, former Secretary of Health, Education and Welfare." The most important problem with the development of the regulation is the constant need to weigh competing equities while resolving complex issues. Implicit in this situation is the need to assess carefully the overall impact of a particular requirement both on the persons protected by the statute and those regulated by it."

Appendix A

**Checklist Used To Determine
Whether Buildings Are Accessible
To The Physically Handicapped**

This checklist is based on the American National Standards Institute guidelines developed to determine whether buildings are accessible to the physically handicapped. In some instances the language of the ANSI Standard was modified to quantify data or questions were added to more completely assess a particular aspect of a building. Other Federal, State, and local/privately developed standards were consulted in making the modifications. The modifications are identified by an asterisk.

Each question requires a "yes", "no", or "not applicable" response. "Not applicable" responses occur where the particular building category under inspection is nonexistent or where the adequacy of that building category is impossible to determine from the building plans, or from questioning/interviewing or observation. Narrative comments and specific measurements requested during the inspections should be included.

Site Development

Yes No N/A

☐ ☐ ☐ Is the grading of the site, even contrary to existing topography, such that approaches to the building can be provided which are substantially level with building entrances?

_____
_____

☐ ☐ ☐ Is there parking within 200 feet of the building entrance?

_____
_____

☐ ☐ ☐ Is any of this parking identified as reserved for use by individuals with physical disabilities?

_____
_____

Yes	No	N/A	
☐	☐	☐	Are there any parking spaces open on one side, allowing room for individuals in wheelchairs or on braces to get in and out of an automobile?
☐	☐	☐	If parking spaces for individuals with physical disabilities are placed between two conventional diagonal or head-on parking spaces, are they at least 12 feet wide?
☐	☐	☐	Is it unnecessary for individuals in wheelchairs or those using braces or crutches to wheel or walk behind parked cars?
☐	☐	☐	Are the parking spaces located to allow persons to get in or out on a level surface?
☐	☐	☐	Is there clear, level, or ramped path (void of curbs) from the parking lot to the building entrances?
☐	☐	☐	Are walks at least 48 inches wide?
☐	☐	☐	Is the walk gradient not greater than 5 percent (1-foot rise in 20 feet)?
☐	☐	☐	Are walks of a continuing common surface, not interrupted by steps or abrupt changes in level?
☐	☐	☐	Wherever walks cross other walks, driveways, or parking lots, do walks blend to a common level?

Yes No N/A

☐ ☐ ☐ Do walks that are elevated have a level platform at the top which is (a) at least 5-by-5 feet if a door swings out onto the platform or toward the walk, or (b) 3-by-5 feet if door does not swing onto the platform?

☐ ☐ ☐ Does the platform extend at least 1 foot beyond each side (inside and outside) of the doorway?

☐ ☐ ☐ Do walks have a surface that is nonslip?

Buildings

Yes No N/A

☐ ☐ ☐ Do ramps have a slope no greater than 8.33 percent, or a 1-foot rise in 12 feet?

☐ ☐ ☐ If ramps have a gradient of more than 5 percent, are handrails provided on at least one side?

☐ ☐ ☐ If handrails are provided are they 32 inches in height measured from the surface of the ramp?

☐ ☐ ☐ Are the surfaces smooth?

☐ ☐ ☐ Do the surfaces extend 1 foot beyond the top and bottom of the ramp?

Yes No N/A

☐ ☐ ☐ Do ramps have a surface that is nonslip?

☐ ☐ ☐ Do ramps have at least 6 feet of straight clearance at the bottom?

☐ ☐ ☐ Do the ramps have level rest areas, a minimum of 5 feet in length, provided at turns?

☐ ☐ ☐ Do ramps that exceed a gradient of 5 percent have level platforms, a minimum of 3 feet in length, at 30-foot intervals?

☐ ☐ ☐ Do ramps that exceed a gradient of 5 percent have level rest areas, a minimum of 5 feet in length, provided at turns?

☐ ☐ ☐ Is at least one primary entrance to the building usable by individuals in wheelchairs? (It is preferable that all or most entrances (exits) should be accessible to and usable by individuals in wheelchairs or other forms of physical disability.)

☐ ☐ ☐ Is at least one entrance usable by individuals in wheelchairs on a level that would make the elevators accessible?

☐ ☐ ☐ Do doors have a clear opening of no less than 32 inches when open?

☐ ☐ ☐ Are doors operable by a single effort? Note: Two leaf doors are usable by those with disabilities unless they operate by single effort, or unless one of the two leaves meets the 32-inch width.

Yes No N/A

☐ ☐ ☐ Is the floor of the doorway level for a distance of 5 feet from the door in the direction it swings?

_____

_____

☐ ☐ ☐ Does the floor of the doorway extend 1 foot beyond each side of door?

_____

_____

☐ ☐ ☐ Does the floor of the doorway extend 3 feet in the direction opposite to the door swing?

_____

_____

☐ ☐ ☐ Is the floor of the doorway at least 5 feet wide?

_____

_____

☐ ☐ ☐ Are sharp inclines and abrupt changes in level avoided at doorsills?

_____

_____

☐ ☐ ☐ Does the speed of door closers allow the use of doors by physically disabled persons?

_____

_____

☐ ☐ ☐ Do steps avoid abrupt nosing? Note: Nosing is the protruding lip at the front edge of steps.

_____

_____

☐ ☐ ☐ Do stairs have handrails 32 inches high as measured from the tread at the face of the riser?

_____

_____

☐ ☐ ☐ Do stairs have at least one handrail that extends at least 18 inches beyond the top and bottom step (parallel to floor or landing, and extension preferably secured to wall to avoid creation of a hazard)?

_____

_____

Yes No N/A

☐ ☐ ☐ Do steps have risers 7 inches or less?
_____
_____

☐ ☐ ☐ Do floors have a nonslip surface?
_____
_____

☐ ☐ ☐ Are floors on each story at a common level or connected by a ramp? (There should be no differences in level between corridor and adjacent rooms).
_____
_____

☐ ☐ ☐ Is there at least one toilet for each sex on each floor with facilities for the physically handicapped?
_____
_____

☐ ☐ ☐ Can physically handicapped persons, particularly those in wheelchairs, enter the restroom?
_____
_____

☐ ☐ ☐ Do toilet rooms have turning space 60-by-60 inches to allow traffic of individuals in wheelchairs?
_____
_____

☐ ☐ ☐ Do toilet rooms have at least one toilet stall that is 3 feet wide?
_____
_____

☐ ☐ ☐ Do toilet rooms have at least one toilet stall that is at least 4 feet, 8 inches (preferably 5 feet) deep?
_____
_____

☐ ☐ ☐ Do toilet rooms have at least one toilet stall that has a door that is 32 inches wide and swings out?
_____
_____

☐ ☐ ☐ Do toilet rooms have at least one toilet stall that has handrails on

Yes No N/A

each side, 33 inches high and parallel to floor, 1 inch in diameter, with 1 inch clearance between rail and wall, fastened securely to the wall at the ends and center? If grab bars are other than parallel, describe.

_____
_____

☐ ☐ ☐ Do toilet rooms have at least one toilet stall that has a clearance of at least 48 inches between the outside wall and the front of the stall entrance?

_____
_____

☐ ☐ ☐ Do toilet rooms have at least one toilet stall that has water closet with seat 20 inches from the floor?

_____
_____

☐ ☐ ☐ Do toilet rooms have lavatories (wash basins) with narrow aprons, which when mounted at standard height are no greater than 34 inches at the top and which have a clearance underneath of 29 inches?

_____
_____

☐ ☐ ☐ Are drain pipes and hot water pipes covered or insulated?

_____
_____

☐ ☐ ☐ Is one mirror at a height as low as possible and no higher than 40 inches above the floor?

_____
_____

☐ ☐ ☐ Is one shelf at a height as low as possible and no higher than 40 inches above the floor?

_____
_____

☐ ☐ ☐ Do toilet rooms for men have wall-mounted urinals with the opening of the basis 19 inches from the floor, or have floor mounted urinals that are level with the main floor of the toilet room?

_____
_____

Yes No N/A

☐ ☐ ☐ Do toilet rooms have towel racks mounted no higher than 40 inches from the floor?

___

☐ ☐ ☐ Are other dispensers mounted no higher than 40 inches from the floor?

___

☐ ☐ ☐ Are disposal units mounted no higher than 40 inches from the floor?

___

☐ ☐ ☐ Are towel racks, towel dispensers and other appropriate disposal units located to the side of the lavatory rather than directly above?

___

☐ ☐ ☐ Is there at least one drinking fountain on each floor for use by the physically handicapped?

___

☐ ☐ ☐ Can persons in wheelchairs wheel up to the water fountain?

___

☐ ☐ ☐ Do water fountains or coolers have up-front spouts and controls?

___

☐ ☐ ☐ Are the water fountains hand operated?

___

☐ ☐ ☐ If coolers are wall mounted, are they hand operated, with basins 36 inches or less from the floor?

___

Yes	No	N/A	
☐	☐	☐	Is there at least one public telephone in each "bank" accessible to physically handicapped persons?
☐	☐	☐	Is the height of the dial from the floor 48 inches or less?
☐	☐	☐	Is the coin slot located 48 inches or less from the floor?
☐	☐	☐	Are there telephones equipped for persons with hearing disabilities?
☐	☐	☐	Are telephones equipped for persons with hearing disabilities identified as such?
☐	☐	☐	If more than a one-story building, are elevators available to the physically handicapped?
☐	☐	☐	Can physically handicapped persons, particularly those in wheelchairs, enter elevators?
☐	☐	☐	Are outside call buttons 48 inches or less from the floor?
☐	☐	☐	Are control buttons inside the elevators 48 inches or less from the floor?
☐	☐	☐	Are the buttons labeled with raised (or indented) letters beside them?

Yes No N/A

☐ ☐ ☐ Are the buttons touch sensitive or easy to push?

☐ ☐ ☐ Is the elevator cab at least 5-by-5 feet?

☐ ☐ ☐ Can a person in a wheelchair facing the rear see floor numbers (by mirror or floor identification number at rear of cab)?

☐ ☐ ☐ Are floors announced orally by recorded devices for the benefit of the blind?

☐ ☐ ☐ Are light switches not more than 48 inches above the floor?

☐ ☐ ☐ Are controls for heating, cooling and ventilation not more than 48 inches above the floor?

☐ ☐ ☐ Are controls for fire alarms and other warning signals not more than 48 inches above the floor?

☐ ☐ ☐ Are controls for draperies and other items of frequent or essential use not more than 48 inches above the floor?

☐ ☐ ☐ Are raised (or recessed) letters or numbers used to identify rooms or offices?

☐ ☐ ☐ Is identification placed on the wall, to the right or left of the door?

Yes No N/A

☐ ☐ ☐ Is such identification placed at a height between 4 feet 6 inches and 5 feet 6 inches, measured from the floor?

☐ ☐ ☐ Are doors that might prove dangerous to a blind person if he were to exit or enter through them (doors not intended for normal use) made quickly identifiable to the touch by knurled door handles or knobs?

☐ ☐ ☐ Are audible warning signals accompanied by simultaneous of those with hearing or sight disabilities?

☐ ☐ ☐ When manholes or access panels are open and in use, or when an open excavation exists on a site, when it is approximate to normal pedestrian traffic, are barricades placed on all open sides at least 8 feet from the hazard, and warning devices installed?

☐ ☐ ☐ Are there no low-hanging door closers that remain within the opening of a doorway, or that protrude hazardously into regular corridors or traffic ways?

☐ ☐ ☐ Are there no low-hanging signs, ceiling lights, fixtures, or similar objects that protrude into regular corridors or traffic ways? (A minimum height of 7 feet, measured from floor is recommended.)

☐ ☐ ☐ Is lighting on ramps adequate?

☐ ☐ ☐ Are exit signs easily identifiable to all disabled persons?

Footnotes

Introduction
1. Department of Health, Education and Welfare. Nondiscrimination on the basis of handicap. *Federal Register,* Vol. 41, no. 96, May 17, 1976.
2. Barbacovi, Don R. and Clelland, Richard W. *Public Law 94-142: Special Education in Transition.* Arlington, Virginia: American Association of School Administrators, 1977.

Chapter I
1. The "Overview of Title V" is paraphrased and slightly modified from Gardner, Bill F. and Minton, Elizabeth B. *Affirmative Action: A Resource Manual for Vocational Rehabilitation.* Morgantown, West Virginia: Research and Training Center, 1976, pp. 11-13.
2. The "Overview of Section 504 Regulation" is paraphrased and slightly modified from Department of Health, Education and Welfare. Nondiscrimination on the basis of handicap. *Federal Register,* Vol. 42, no. 86, May 4, 1977, p. 22677.

Chapter II
1. Schneider, Benjamin. *Staffing Organizations.* Pacific Palisades, California: Goodyear Publishing Co., Inc., 1976, p. 3.
2. Schneider, Benjamin, p. 3.
3. Schneider, Benjamin, p. 5.
4. Gardner, J. N. *Excellence: Can We Be Equal and Excellent Too!* New York, New York: Harper, 1961, p. 18.
5. The "Developmental History of Section 504 Regulation: Legislative History" is paraphrased and slightly modified from Gardner, Bill F. and Minton, Elizabeth B., pp. 7-10.
6. Weckstein, P. Legal challenges to educational testing practices. *Inequality in Education,* 1973, *15,* p. 92.
7. Weckstein, P., p. 92.
8. *Bridgeport Guardians, Inc. v. Members of the Bridgeport Civil Service Commission.* 354 F. Supp. 778 (1973), pp. 778-779.
9. *Griggs v. Duke Power Co.* 401 U.S. 424 (1971), p. 158.
10. *Griggs v. Duke Power Co.,* p. 159.
11. *Griggs v. Duke Power Co.,* p. 160.
12. *Bridgeport Guardians, Inc. v. Members of the Bridgeport Civil Service Commission,* p. 780.

13. *Griggs v. Duke Power Co.*, p. 164.
14. *Griggs v. Duke Power Co.*, p. 164.
15. Weckstein, P., p. 92.
16. *Arrington v. Massachusetts Bay Transportation Authority.* 306 F. Supp. 1355 (1969), p. 1355.
17. *Baker v. Columbus Municipal Separate School District.* 462 F. 2d 112 (1972), p. 114.
18. Weckstein, P., p. 93.
19. *Armstead v. Starkville Municipal Separate School District.* 461 F. 2d 276 (1972), p. 276.
20. Weckstein, P., p. 93.
21. Weckstein, P., p. 93.
22. Weckstein, P., p. 93.
23. *United States v. Georgia Power Company.* 474 F. 2d 418 (1973), pp. 906-907.
24. *United States v. Georgia Power Company,* p. 911.
25. *United States v. Georgia Power Company,* p. 912.
26. *United States v. Georgia Power Company,* pp. 912-916.
27. Weckstein, P., p. 94.
28. *Chance v. Board of Examiners and Board of Education of City of New York.* 330 F. Supp. 203 (1971), p. 216.
29. *Fowler v. Schwarzwalder.* 351 F. Supp. 721 (1972), p. 724.
30. *Fowler v. Schwarzwalder,* p. 725.
31. *Fowler v. Schwarzwalder,* p. 727.
32. *United States v. Jacksonville Terminal Company.* 451 F. 2d 418 (1971), p. 456.
33. Weckstein, P., p. 94.
34. Weckstein, P., p. 94.
35. *Baker v. Columbus Municipal Separate School District,* p. 114.
36. The "Delineation of Specific Regulatory Requirements" is paraphrased and slightly modified from Department of Health, Education and Welfare. Nondiscrimination on the basis of handicap. *Federal Register,* Vol. 42, no. 86, May 4, 1977, pp. 22678-22681.
37. *Equal Employment Opportunity Commission.* Guidelines on employment selection procedures. Federal Register, Vol. 35, 1970, pp. 12333-12336.
38. Fox, David J. *The Research Process in Education.* New York, New York: Holt, Rinehart and Winston, Inc., 1969, p. 367.
39. Fox, David J., p. 353.
40. Borich, Gary D. Introduction to roles and contexts, in Borich, Gary D. (Ed.) *Evaluating Educational Programs and Products.* Englewood Cliffs, New Jersey: Educational Technology Publications, 1974, p. 28.
41. Borich, Gary D., p. 28.
42. Borich, Gary D., p. 28.
43. Borich, Gary D., p. 29.
44. Borich, Gary D., p. 29.
45. Borich, Gary D., p. 29.

46. Borich, Gary D., p. 30.
47. Worthen, Blaine R. and Sanders, James R. (Eds.) *Educational Evaluation: Theory and Practice.* Belmont, California: Wadsworth Publishing Co., Inc., 1973, pp. 143-148.
48. Worthen, Blaine R. and Sanders, James R., p. 144.
49. The "Job Analysis: What it is and its Uses" is paraphrased and slightly modified from U.S. Department of Labor, Manpower Administration. *Handbook for Analyzing Jobs.* Washington, D.C.: U.S. Government Printing Office, 1972, p. 1.
50. The "Concepts and Principles in Job Analysis" is paraphrased and slightly modified from U.S. Department of Labor, Manpower Administration, pp. 3-10.
51. Executive Office of the President, Bureau of the Budget. *Standard Industrial Classification Manual.* Washington, D.C.: U.S. Government Printing Office, 1967.
52. U.S. Department of Health, Education and Welfare. *Standard Terminology for Curriculum and Instruction in Local and State School Systems.* Washington, D.C.: U.S. Government Printing Office, 1970.
53. Bingham, W. V. *Aptitudes and Aptitude Testing.* New York, New York: Harper and Brothers, 1937.
54. Fox, David J., p. 646.
55. Fox, David J., p. 565.
56. Fox, David J., p. 543.
57. Fox, David J., p. 521.
58. U.S. Department of Labor, Manpower Administration. *Handbook for Analyzing Jobs.* Washington, D.C.: U.S. Government Printing Office, 1972.
59. O'Neill, David M. Discrimination against handicapped persons: the costs, benefits and economic impact of implementing Section 504 of the Rehabilitation Act of 1973 covering recipients of HEW financial assistance. *Federal Register,* Vol. 41, no. 96, May 17, 1976.

Chapter III

1. Architectural and Transportation Barriers Compliance Board. *First report of the architectural and transportation barriers compliance board to the Congress of the United States.* Washington, D.C.: United States Department of Health, Education and Welfare, 1974.
2. The "Developmental History of Section 504 Regulation: Legislative History" is paraphrased and slightly modified from Comptroller General of the United States. *Further action needed to make all public buildings accessible to the physically handicapped,* 1975.
3. American National Standards Institute, Inc. *Specification for making buildings and facilities accessible to and usable by, the physically handicapped.* New York, New York: American National Standard Institute, Inc., 1961.
4. The "Developmental History of Section 504 Regulation: Judicial History" is paraphrased and slightly modified from Rigdon, Louis T. *Civil Rights.* Awareness paper prepared for the White House Conference on Handicapped Individuals. U.S. Department of Health, Education and Welfare, Office of Human Development, 1976.
5. The "Delineation of Specific Regulatory Requirements" is paraphrased and slightly modified from Department of Health, Education and Welfare. Nondis-

crimination on the basis of handicap. *Federal Register,* Vol. 42, no. 86, May 4, 1977, p. 22681.
6. Yavorsky, Diane K. *Discrepancy Evaluation: A Practitioner's Guide.* University of Virginia: Evaluation Research Center, 1976, p. 3.
7. Yavorsky, Diane K., p. 3.
8. Developed from Educational Research Services, Inc. *Barrier-Free School Facilities for Handicapped Students.* Arlington, Virginia: Educational Research Service, Inc., 1977.
9. Educational Research Service, Inc., p. 60.
10. Educational Research Service, Inc., p. 61-62.
11. Educational Research Service, Inc., p. 50.
12. Comptroller General of the United States, Appendix II, pp. 95-107.
13. Paraphrased and slightly modified from O'Neill, David M., pp. 21-30.

Chapter IV

1. National Association of State Directors of Special Education and Pottinger and Company Consultants. *The Rehabilitation Act: An Analysis of the Section 504 Regulation and Its Implications for State and Local Education Agencies.* Washington, D.C.: National Association of State Directors of Special Education, 1977.
2. National Association of State Directors of Special Education. *Section 504/P.L. 94-142: A Comparison of Selected Provisions of the Proposed Regulations for Section 504 of the Vocational Rehabilitation Act of 1974 and Selected Provisions of P.L. 94-142, The Education for All Handicapped Childrens Act of 1975.* Washington, D.C.: National Association of State Directors of Special Education, 1976.

References

A substantial number of references were used for *Public Law 94-142: Special Education in Transition* and *Section 504: Civil Rights for the Handicapped*. The author, therefore, recommends that public school administrators review the following works.

American Society of Landscape Architects Foundation and U.S. Department of Housing and Urban Development, Office of Policy Development and Research. *Barrier Free Site Design*. Washington, D.C.: U.S. Government Printing Office, 1976.

Kaufman, M. J., Gottlieb, J, Agard, J. A., and Kukic, M. B. Mainstreaming: Toward an explication of the construct. *Focus on Exceptional Children, 7,* 1975.

Kliment, S. A. Into the Mainstream: *A Syllabus for a Barrier-Free Environment*. Washington, D.C.: American Institute of Architects and Rehabilitation Services Administration of the U.S. Department of Health, Education and Welfare, U.S. Government Printing Office. (No Date)

Kunder, Linda H. *Barrier-Free School Facilities for Handicapped Students*. Arlington, Virginia: Educational Research Service, Inc., 1977. Note: The author strongly recommends the Educational Research Service document. It is not only extensive in coverage, but has an excellent annotated reference list and selected bibliography.

Meyer, E. L., Vergason, G. A., and Whelan, R. J. (Eds.) *Strategies for Teaching Exceptional Children*. Denver, Colorado: Love Publishing Co., 1972.

National Association of State Directors of Special Education. *Functions of the Placement Committee in Special Education*. Washington, D.C.: NASDSE, 1976.

Weintraub, F., Abeson, A., Ballard, J., and LaVor, M. (Eds.) *Public Policy and the Education of Exceptional Children*. Reston, Virginia: The Council for Exceptional Children, 1976.

About the Author

Dr. Richard W. Clelland is currently working with the New Mexico Teacher Education/Special Education Dissemination Project in Washington, D.C. From the University of Florida, Dr. Clelland received his B.A. degree in secondary education, M.A. degree in mental retardation, and Ed. D. in special education administration. Following one year as a special class teacher of the educable mentally retarded at the elementary school level in Miami, Florida, he was employed two years as a teacher of the educable mentally retarded with the Putnam County Public Schools, Palatka, Florida. During 1976-1977 Dr. Clelland worked as an University Council for Educational Administration National Level Intern. As a National Level Intern, Dr. Clelland provided technical assistance to the member cities of the Council of the Great City Schools and the American Association of School Administrators, as well as presented papers at a wide variety of national conferences.